# Memories Of Lockdown

3rd book of the trilogy

Copyright © 2024 Rosanne Gallagher

All rights reserved. No part of this publication may be reproduced or transmitted in any form or by any means, electronic or mechanical including photocopying, recording or any information storage or retrieval system, without prior permission in writing from the publishers.

The right of Rosanne Gallagher to be identified as the author of this work has been asserted by her in accordance with the Copyright, Designs and Patents Act 1988

First published in the United Kingdom in 2024 by
The Choir Press

ISBN: 978-1-78963-440-2

Cover design by Bob Hellyer
www.BobHellyer.art
Typeset by Phoenix Media
www.phoenixmediadesign.com

"Thank you to my wonderful family and friends - without all of you there would be no book"

## Introduction

Another year on and I have continued to watch families and friends divide, and new relationships and friendship groups form and strengthen. I have continued to collect unique stories from ordinary people who have chosen to share their views and experiences with us, and it has been consistently interesting to see how different our perceptions have been over the last three years and how differently we have dealt with changing circumstances in the best way we could individually, making choices and decisions to get through these times and go forward.

People choosing who they want to share their life with, where and how they want to live; there's so much disillusionment with the very foundations people used to look up to and respect, but now, on some level, do not trust. Visions for the future have changed and many find themselves on new paths.

Community is becoming important again as we recognise we each have a piece of the puzzle and we need each other to put that puzzle together as we navigate one of the greatest changes the world has ever seen.

Book three is a continuation of stories from some of my wonderful writers in Books One & Two, and new writers who have joined us from New Zealand, Spain, Northern Ireland, the UK and the USA - stories bringing news of how people have found the last year with their thoughts, views and opinions.

Throughout these years I have maintained a great respect for each person and the choices they have made - the whole point of my trilogy was, and is, to create more understanding between us all by reading each other's stories and recognising that "We don't all see things the same way."

I hope you enjoy the stories as much as I have!

'It's All About The Children'

## Rosanne

Another year has passed in a flash and I find myself looking back, not just over the past year, but over the past 3 years since I had my first idea for this 'Memories Trilogy'. Here is my story and apologies in advance if I repeat anything I have already said in the first books...

After Mum died and Christmas 2019 passed, Dad started putting all his energies into promoting his book 'Memories of a Different World' and I wanted to help him with whatever would give him a reason to get up in the morning!

We had spent the winter months applying for his new passport; he had decided he must renew his passport, and after many trips back and forth between him and the local post office, because with his unsteady hand he found it very hard to 'sign within the square', we eventually got his new passport. Although the probability was that he would never use it I was determined to help him get it to give him 'hope'.

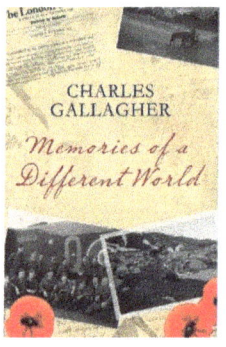

Back to his book - we started planning a 'Tour' of Care Homes as Dad thought they would be a good audience for his talk and would generate sales!

With the help of my dear friend 'Linda' who wrote in Book 2, we went to our first 'Care Home Talk' in early February. It was a great success and my wonderful Dad gained strength and so enjoyed meeting and talking to new people - it made me happy to see him with some renewed interest and enthusiasm, and together we were planning our next talks when lockdown struck. When I look back it breaks my heart to think of him alone, without Mum, without daily visitors, sitting in his room day after day until he died on Christmas Eve and finally joined Mum again. I chose not to attend my Dad's funeral with the government rules of 30 people, masks and sitting apart... and instead went to exactly where he would  have expected to see me that day - high on the cliffs of Dorset in one of our shared favourite places in the World!

I had returned to my home in Spain during the time I wasn't allowed to see Dad in the first lockdown, and flew back to the UK as soon as I could visit him again. I was then allowed to see him, at a distance, for a couple of hours a week. I spoke to him on the phone every day and we planned for the future - anything to give him hope and a little joy in his heart.

On my last visit I was 'allowed' to sit with him which gave me the opportunity I had been longing for... to hold his hand, give him a hug and a kiss. I knew this would be our last time together in this lifetime and I told him how much I loved him and what a wonderful father he'd been; I talked through his whole life with him and on some level I was sure he heard every word - how I got up and left him I will never know, but I did.

Whether I will ever truly forgive the powers that kept me at a distance from my father I am not sure; at this moment, thinking of those that made the rules partying and

ignoring their own rules, I think not.

However, as I believe 'forgiveness' is, and will be, a major part of our way forward maybe I will reach that, what seems now, unattainable height.

I have been working through my grief at the loss of my parents and the circumstance of Dad's passing and recently in a conversation the word 'helplessness' came up and I recognised it. I had felt so helpless not being able to take Dad home to look after him and in those last months with my parents Dad had re-written his Will. He had thought so deeply about it and was so pleased when he finally handed it to his solicitor; at that time not knowing it would never be signed and actioned. He had chosen so carefully each and every 'thing' he wanted his children and grandchildren to have, but then Mum died and after that we never talked about his Will again. Somehow, anything after Mum's death seemed trivial and I felt that any mention of a change in his Will at that time would have led to his mental health being assessed and that would have been too terrible. So I left it, and knowing that he thought it was in order gave me comfort. In his passing it didn't matter but during that time it felt so wrong. Again I had felt helpless.

I have the greatest gift - the memories... when my children were young I used to fly over from Spain to spend long summers with my parents, and we had spent so much time together in the last 13 or so years of their lives. All the wonderful hours, days, weeks of conversations, shared memories, laughing, eating, drinking and forming a deeper bond, friendship and love, just being together.

*Rosanne*

I am forever grateful for those special times when I sat among my family - my parents, children and grandchildren, just being... with the foundation of a deep mutual love and respect. Four generations with so much to share, from the wisdom and experience of the elders to the wisdom and dreams of the young. In my heart forever.

I continue to follow my heart and it continues to lead me well. This year has been another year of exploring and creating my new life, assessing and re-assessing everything and everyone I encounter and trusting that the Universe has got my back!

In the last years I have learnt so much and feel so much stronger for it - things make more sense now - my life has more purpose. I have joined many dots and within this learning I have experienced joy, grief, peace, loneliness, patience, acceptance, mourning, and many other emotions. It has been quite a ride but one that I am glad I had the opportunity to jump on. It has helped me to accept the many things I have lost; my dearest parents in death, the family I thought I had, my previous home and life. Letting go of old certainties - it's a hard and lonely journey but in a strange way it sets you free. It makes you reevaluate your life and relationships, rethink what really matters, and let go of things and people that don't make you happy or serve your highest purpose.

We are so much stronger than we think and I welcome into my life the gift of my new soul family - my beautiful new friends who shine like diamonds - and I thank those who caused me the most unhappiness for the lessons they taught me - indeed, they were my greatest teachers.

I believe we continue to experience an enormous time of change and transition - relationships, jobs, friendships, values, our whole way of life, and personally I welcome and embrace the change.

I have learnt from the wonderful Pam Gregory (astrologer) how to 'step back onto my eagle's perch and observe' when things don't go quite as I wanted or expected them to, when the world has apparently lost its way, when I see chaos and confusion, unreasonable behaviour and lack of common sense, and this has undoubtedly been one of the best lessons to help me through these times. 'Forever grateful Pam'. She is such an inspiration to so many.

I observe, feel the emotion, make my decision and follow my heart. It feels good and is very empowering. I recognise a deep knowing, a knowing that has always been there which in previous times was labelled as a free-spirit, rebellious, non-conformist or just plain annoying and awkward!

The Winter, full of lovely family moments and many wonderful walks with the dogs in the beautiful nature we have all around us whilst keeping the continuity of local projects alive which was and is very exciting.

With the Spring, as ever, we saw new life all around which is always a true and beautiful 'wonder' to me - the power of nature and how utterly inspiring it is. The expectancy and hope as the days got longer and our dreams of Summer came closer.

One of my projects, the 'Energy Enhancement System' based on frequency energy healing, arrived in the UK and a group of us travelled to London from Glastonbury; an unforgettable experience, an unforgettable day shared with a group of wonderful friends. We came home even more sure and determined to turn our dream of creating a Healing Centre in Glastonbury into a reality; by this time next year I anticipate that our doors will be open and I'll be telling you all about it in the next book! Perhaps some of you will come and visit!

Another project I am involved with is the PHA - People's Health Alliance - the PHA has now spread across the UK and throughout 30+ countries across the world. The concept is offering an alternative Health Service so that people become more informed and have a choice in how they wish to deal with their health.

I also assist a local weekly grief/loss support group, run by my lovely friend Carol whose poem dedicated to our 'elders' is in this book; the group gives people the opportunity to drop in and have a cup of tea with us, talk if they wish, make new friends and feel part of the community. After the last years there are many people who still feel very alone and everyone has lost something or someone.

All the seasons are beautiful in this big abundant garden known as Somerset and although the weather over the summer months wasn't consistently full of sunshine, I made the most of the long light days and enjoyed many cups of tea and hours of chatting and planning the future we want to see with friends and dogs, in, amongst other places, the Abbey Gardens of Glastonbury - a truly magical place to walk barefoot in nature.

Drives down to the coasts of Dorset and Devon with my dear friend Helen - so very beautiful - the feel of the sand underfoot, shingle, rippling waves, sounds of the sea and cups of tea - china teapots - children's voices - dogs running free - close your eyes and you're anywhere you want to be!

The year has whizzed by so quickly, it's hard to imagine that we are almost in November and by the time this book goes to print it will be early December and Christmas again!

In the last two books I talked about being given the 'Gift of Time' and over the past year I have learnt how to give myself the 'Gift of Time' as and when I need to step back and spend time alone, something I've never done before and am grateful for.

In 2020 when Covid jumped onto the stage and into the spotlight, we heard of nothing else for a very long time! The world closed down - the bottom of our world dropped out and many of us fell through; we went into freefall for a minute, an hour, a day, a week, a month, a year, and some are still there, totally confused about what is going on now and what the future may hold.

We have all had to deal with it in our own way and make our individual choices - I choose to seize the opportunity and help to make the world a better place.

Do you remember back in 1991 Michael Jackson was singing about just that? Whatever you or I thought about him is irrelevant… his video of 'Heal The World' was pretty good! The children's faces, the words and the intention of inspiring worldwide peace, love and tolerance, by showing a diverse group of children united in their abilities to love unconditionally and their wishes for a brighter future.

Not a bad goal, and on the very bright side, I think we are already seeing it. It's up to each one of us - 'We are the Change.'

The old way hasn't worked for a long time and I think our future is more exciting than any of us can imagine with all the new innovative thinkers and creators out there.

I have so enjoyed my journey with these three books - we all have a story to tell and I will be sharing more stories of mine and of others in the years to come...

So let's all be the hero of our own story, believe in ourselves and make our dreams come true for us and those around us. Realise our soul purpose individually and collectively, the purpose of what we are really here to do. Let's break ancestral and generational patterns that do not serve us and 'Let Go With Love and Compassion'.

It's all exactly as it's meant to be and I will always live in wonderment and love... forever optimistic. 💜

"Wonderment & Love"

# Jill from Noosa, Australia

As I wrote my story last year, my husband and I were on our way up to see our daughter in Cairns and then joined by my son, his partner and our adorable little grandson for our first family holiday since before Covid. We had a wonderful happy time all being together again and there was little talk of the big C.

On our return I was contacted by a colleague to ask if I would cover her Monday shifts for a while as she had injured her back. The mandates for health care workers had not been completely lifted at that stage but you were allowed to work if no one else was available for the shift, and so I came out of my forced retirement and went back to my previous role as a support worker for a client I'd worked with for seven years previously.

Another parent also contacted me on occasions when unable to get other support and so my complete retirement was rather short lived... however to be honest it was very welcome to not only keep contact with such long-standing clients, but with the cost of living skyrocketing out of control it was great to be able to supplement our pension.

What I did find ironic though was that I had previously not been allowed to continue working as I had chosen not to be vaccinated. My personal experience was knowing many people who had suffered bad side affects having had the vaccine, and others, who, like myself had experienced Covid already.

However, one of my client's mothers became ill with Covid and I was the only person who would work at the house even though the other members of the team had been vaccinated.

Around the same time as I returned from my holiday I had an email from our real estate agent to say the rental house we had been in for eleven years had been purchased along with the house next door and was to be demolished. We were given until end of February to find somewhere else to live. We decided to just enjoy Christmas and start looking for a new home afterwards.

Noosa is a very busy holiday destination and a lot of the rental pool has been used for Airbnb. Also during the pandemic many of the houses owned by southerners as a second home had now become people's first home.

I think the fact that the lockdowns in Victoria and New South Wales had been so much stricter than in Queensland, we had a huge influx of work from home, and wealthier people who realised what a great climate and lifestyle we enjoyed, decided to become permanent. The knock-on effect was dramatic.

Lots of businesses were unable to get staff as more and more long time locals were forced out of town unable to afford the astronomical rents and the ever escalating price of properties. The Facebook community page was flooded with desperate people looking for rentals and stories of families now having to live in cars. There were many similar scenarios to ours where long-term tenants were being forced out so houses could be supposedly renovated or sold, and then the rents literally going up by hundreds of dollars a week.

Many elderly have been forced to couch surf from friend to friend or move in with family and give up all their possessions. Suicide rates and mental health issues have in turn grown beyond comprehension.

As for us, about 6 weeks before our lease expired I contacted the real estate agent to ask their expectation of cleaning when we vacated. Obviously we were not going to leave the house and garden a mess, but our landlady had previously said that due to the house either being renovated or knocked down there was no need for a full bond clean; i.e. carpets etc. being cleaned, walls, doors and windows scrubbed .

The reply was that they wanted it left in tip-top condition as although, at that stage, they only had development approval from the council, there was a chance the house would be rented out again.

As we were having great difficulty ourselves finding anywhere I asked if we could have a week by week agreement and stay on for a while. Just ten days before our move out date they replied to say no. So much to our annoyance we paid out $500 for the carpets to be professionally cleaned and the gardens done.

The house then stood empty for five months, by which time the gardens were completely overgrown and it was then demolished.

So with only just over a week to go I put out a call on Facebook asking if any friends knew of anywhere we could go, even if only for a short period. Luckily I had trusted that we would be looked after and I got a reply from someone I had worked with a few years previously who said they had an acreage property with a second house on that we were able to have for as long as needed. It was about a forty minute drive away, didn't have a garage for all my husbands tools, bikes etc, but we were so very grateful to still have a roof over our heads especially when sadly so many people haven't had the same good fortune as ourselves.

It has changed our lifestyle completely and we now spend a lot more time in the car going backwards and forwards, but a plus has been that we are only ten minutes away from our grandson. We hope at some stage to move back closer to town, but although there are now more houses becoming available the prices are literally double what they used to be and the mortgage rates have gone up and up - so we are hoping for something to change.

As I write my final little story I am travelling to the UK for the first time in five years to catch up with my family for two weeks, before going to Sweden with the other side of my family to meet my nephew of 18 months.

My brother is married to a Swedish lady and since brexit is unable to travel out of the country until his visa is granted as he then might not be allowed back in... oh how times have changed over these last few years.

The Covid pandemic has changed everybody's life in some way or another, some in good ways and some not so good... my personal feeling is that the world we lived in was never ever what we thought it was... the corruption and manipulation that has come to light has awakened many and is still doing so.

However, I am still trusting in better times and as always live by the rule that 'Love Is The Answer.'

# Ken Strauss

Just like the rest of you, I didn't want to die of Covid. But I was just the kind of person who might—elderly (late 60's), hypertensive and male. That was February, 2020, and I was in Bergamo, Italy—soon to be the European epicenter of the pandemic.

During the third week of that month the virus was moving stealthfully through the smaller towns of Lombardy, ready to pounce on Bergamo. The local newspaper there still devoted only two pages a day to obituaries. That was soon to change.

Remember how little we knew back then. We knew the virus had come out of China. We knew that in some hospitals in Wuhan, 1 out of 5 people who'd caught it, died, and they died quickly, drowning in their own lung secretions, often in a day or two. We knew that the Chinese doctor who'd alerted the world to the peril, a healthy young man, had himself died.

And now suddenly it was in Italy.

It was out there somewhere but we didn't know where. We had no idea how to avoid it. We'd refuse to go to public loos for fear of getting infected by the toilet seat or the sink. We'd scrub our veggies, even our cereal boxes. We debated whether bleach was better than cleanser or soap. It was only later we learned that transmission is largely an aerosol affair and not by surface contact.

But we did know some things, and doctors, like myself, knew a bit more than the general public because we had heard about SARS and MIRS. Those were frightening little epidemics with devastating morbidity and mortality which occurred locally in Asia and the Middle East during the early and middle aughts (decade 2000 to 2009) And the Chinese virus now spreading across Italy was the same kind of coronavirus. Just that word made me shudder.

I didn't want to die from it and was determined not to go to a hospital or to be intubated. So I bought oxygen for home use… not in tanks since they are quickly depleted, but using a new device which extracts oxygen from the air. 'Oxygen concentrators' start at about £400 and provide a flow of oxygen indefinitely, drawn and purified from ambient air. I ordered one of these from California along with tubing, a nasal cannula and a pulse oximeter. The latter is a device you wear on your fingertip which measures the concentration of oxygen in the blood. It gives you the earliest signal that Covid is moving into the stage that can kill you, when the 'O2 sat' (oxygen saturation) falls below 80%.

Then I also stocked up on the medications we knew at that time to be essential: an oral anticoagulant to thin the blood and prevent Covid clots and microclots (one of the chief ways the virus kills), a glucocorticoid (like cortisone or hydrocortisone) to prevent the hyper-intense immune reaction which fills the lungs with inflammatory cells and finally, paracetamol for symptomatic relief of pain and headache. That was all we knew to be effective then and, ironically, remains largely what we know today to be effective.

Now I had everything I might receive in a hospital. I wasn't afraid of the hospital. I continued to work there, but I didn't want to die there. I wanted what every patient dying in hospital wants— to be at home, to have the luxury of passing away in one's own bed. I didn't want to be awakened in the middle of the night by someone taking my vitals, to be super-infected with one of those nosocomial germs, to have all that hustle and bustle around me when I needed to concentrate on dying with dignity, on doing my last great task in life with serenity. Also I'm a widower and didn't want to burden others.

So I got my papers in order, put them all in one leather case. The deed to my house, list of all my property, numbers of bank accounts. I made sure my will was updated and in three languages, English, Spanish and French. (My children would have to file papers in Belgium, Spain and the USA). I left detailed instructions, step by step, how to know I was truly dead, the doctor to call to certify my death, what funeral home to call, how I wanted the service conducted, what readings, what hymns. I left the number of my accountant, my lawyer, my banker.

I sat down with my children and went over all these papers, talked to them calmly about exactly what to do and when. I showed them how the oxygen concentrator worked, how to turn it on and off, how to put on a nasal canula in case they needed it themselves. Everyone was relieved. We had a good laugh and a stiff drink at the end. Everyone went away smiling.

In the end all of this went unused, the oxygen and the meds. I still have the machine and the stocks... still in their boxes. The briefcase with all the papers is still by my bed. I did get Covid three times, but only after I'd been vaccinated. Each time the infection ran a mild to moderate course which didn't necessitate life-saving measures. Which brings me to quarantines and vaccines. We live in an age of mistrust. It used to be only neurotics believed in conspiracies and only the lunatic fringe believed in global conspiracies. Now that's become mainstream. Nowadays you're seen as naive and misguided if you trust in institutions or believe the majority of people are actually out to improve the world and help their neighbours rather than rip them off. Even our most humane friends say, 'I believe in individuals but not in institutions', but what are institutions except a group of individuals who have committed themselves to a cause.

Anyway, when the history of Covid is written 50 or 100 years from now I predict the use of quarantine and vaccines will be seen as critical heroic steps that prevented disaster. What disaster, you may wonder? In those early days, just after Wuhan was devastated, and then Lombardy and then Spain, we knew one thing with rather terrifying certainty. We knew the case/mortality rate; that means how many of those who get infected with Covid actually die. In late March and early April 2020 we already knew that number. It came to us from Wuhan and Lombardy. It was 2%.

Two out of every hundred persons with Covid died, before vaccines and quarantine. That's lower than SARS, lower than MIRS and lower than the Spanish flu of 1918-1919. But it's still a rather staggering number when you consider the world population of nearly 8 billion.

What does the case/mortality rate mean? It means that if you do nothing, you just let the virus rip (as some countries, including the UK, were initially tempted to do) it will infect everyone in the world, (since no one had immunity and the virus is highly communicable) and 2% of those infected will die. So let's do the maths. What's 2% of 8 billion? One hundred and sixty million! Let's say that another way. If we'd just let Covid rip—not taken the measures of social distancing, masking, quarantine and warp-speed vaccination development then jabbing then boosting—160,000,000 people would have died.

I can hear someone sniggering, poo-pooing, scratching his head in disbelief. Again, we live in an age of distrust. And I'm a doctor, plus a white, straight male, so obviously I'm just the kind of person you should never trust.

But we also live in an age of ignorance. We just don't believe such a thing could happen. We don't realize it's happened before. Could a virus kill, in a lightning bolt of time—a few weeks at most—the equivalent of the entire population of the United Kingdom, times two? 'No way,' our doubting Thomas shakes his head. But consider 1918. How many people did that influenza virus (mistakenly called the 'Spanish flu') kill? Well, no one knows for sure because they never counted the dead in India or China, even then the most populous countries in the world. But extrapolating from the statistics we do have, which are quite reliable, it appears that 100,000,000 people died. One hundred million! That was at a time when there were less than 2 billion people on the globe, not 8, and they died quickly. They were often well in the morning, had a sore throat at noon, were bedridden in the afternoon and dead before sundown - and the virus had a special trophism for the young. That means it killed teens and young adults by preference. Troopships of Canadian soldiers leaving the trenches of WW1, which had just ended, would slip hundreds of dead bodies into the sea every day, all victims of the virus. You could track the ship for hundreds of miles by the floating bodies. They'd arrive back in Newfoundland after a 10 day voyage with only half the 6000 soldiers they started with. When it was done the Spanish flu had killed more people than all of WW1—by several orders of magnitude, but who remembers that today? People remember wars, they forget pandemics.

So it has happened. It has devastated humanity before, and, it would have happened again. We were saved. How? By those simple rules: stay at home, only go out for food and medicines, stand two meters apart, wash your hands, wear a mask and finally…take the jab… then the booster. That saved us! No one country got it exactly right, there were starts and stops, wrong turns, reversals and contradictions - but remember, we didn't know shit at that time. Still, that's the miracle we've just lived through and most of us don't even realize it. Most people are so busy resenting the nuisance of these measures or speculating whether it was all a hoax or raving that big pharma fleeced us to realize we've just lived through a miracle. How many actually died? Well, best estimates are that, to date, 7 million people have died of Covid worldwide. That's probably something of an underestimate and, of course, every one of those deaths was a tragedy. Every family loss was horrible. And almost all those 7 million would still be alive today but for Covid. But 7 million is a far, far cry from 160 million, and it would have happened. Anyone who doubts that just hasn't looked carefully at what was happening during the first two months of 2020 in central China, in the hospitals and emergency rooms and intensive care wards of countless hospitals around Wuhan. Anyone who doubts it wasn't, like I was, in Bergamo Italy in March and April 2020 and saw the obituary notices go from an average of 2 pages a day in the newspaper to 60 pages!!! A 30-fold increase in 1 week. The scythe of death slashing through an entire generation of Italians (most my age) in the twinkling of an eye. That would have happened worldwide… and it didn't. And it was a miracle. A modern medical miracle.

Those of us in the medical profession just shake our head at smart people, sensible people, well-informed people who deny the efficacy of vaccines, who refuse to take the Covid vaccine claiming their own immune system is strong enough to fight off the virus or that they don't trust the vaccine development process or the developers. Parents who wouldn't dream of not vaccinating their own children against all the childhood diseases, say these things about the Covid vaccine. They say it was developed too fast, wasn't tested adequately, was only a money-making scam. These are smart people who trust that others will drive on the correct side of the road, that the food they buy at the supermarket is safe to eat, that the bills they carry in their wallet will be accepted as valid tender of custom... all elements of trust... all the vital glue of trust that holds our civilization together. These are the same people who believe they could be harmed by a Covid jab, that claim clinical studies involving 400,000 subjects (in which no additional injury was noted after vaccination) are not reliable, and even wonder whether someone hasn't nefariously slipped a chip into the vaccine vials.

We've discussed this as doctors... we've wondered what's happened to lead us to such a confused, contradictory and counter-productive mindset. One doctor asked me whether if we could take people back for a week to Victorian times and let them see all the children dying before their fifth birthday of diseases like measles, rubella, smallpox... whether that would make a difference in the way they view vaccines, or what if we explained to people the nature of viruses. How they arise, mutate, hijack our cells and intercalate their own genes into our DNA. Tell them how the RNA and DNA vaccine platforms work. How this marvellous vehicle, as wonderful and complex as the Saturn rocket, works. Then explain how the human immune system processes inert viral antigens to make antibodies that protect you. The miracle of vaccines. The most effective medical tool ever invented. Would people finally change their mindset? I doubt it, but how can I blame them? I'm just as silly about other things. Just as blind. We are a silly race. Blindness is comforting when everyone else is blind. Willful blindness is a salve when you're really too afraid to see.

## Alison from Brightlingsea, UK

So, the first lockdown was upon us. The weather was sunny and warm, and for many it was good to be in the garden, catching up on jobs unless you were trapped in a flat for days on end.

During this time my father had a bad fall. While my father is known for his strength of spirit and played it down, it was clear I needed to support him, but lockdown restrictions were in place. While many may disagree with my actions, I visited my father and cared for him. He recovered well, but many elderly, especially those with dementia were very confused by the lockdown policy, and became more isolated and frail as a result.

After a few months of 'freedom', my husband, Mick and I had a holiday at St. Abbs, a small village on the north east coast of Scotland, it was Mick's favourite place. The weather was kind and he visibly soaked up the harbour scene with the seagulls overhead, they always reminded him of St. Abbs.

On our return, I sensed something wasn't quite right with his health, but he was a private man keeping his thoughts to himself.

Then came the second lockdown, restrictions for everything in place again. I remember Mick ringing the surgery to see a doctor (he must have realised he was ill), only to be given a prescription over the phone. He said "I know what they are saying but it's not that."

By Christmas my father had been admitted to hospital with acute kidney trauma. I was told the prognosis was poor, but lockdown meant no visitors. My father miraculously recovered sometime later.

After Christmas, Mick became unwell with breathing difficulties. I remember staying up with him the night before he was admitted to hospital, trying to reassure him he'd be ok while ignoring the oximeter readings. The ambulance arrived, and after deliberations the paramedics decided he should go to hospital, saying he'll be home soon, just some oxygen and antibiotics. I really thought Mick would be back soon, I let the paramedics do their job and never had the opportunity to say 'goodbye'.

My father was still in hospital and now Mick was too, and I couldn't see either of them.

I remember my son driving to the hospital. He knew the hospital ward where his Dad was. It was a ground floor ward and he was desperately hoping he would get a glimpse of his Dad. He had written a sign to hold up at the window "We love you Dad" but, sadly he just couldn't find him.

As lockdown restrictions stopped all visits, the 7pm phone update from the doctors was nerve racking; trying to relay some positive news to my children when there really wasn't any, was so hard. Eventually the dreaded call came very early one morning, Mick was back in ICU on a ventilator. After about a week I received a call from ICU, nothing more could be done and I made the decision to turn off the ventilator.

But what followed was one of the most difficult decisions I have ever made. I could say goodbye, but I would need to quarantine just when I needed support. Only two people could be with Mick as he passed. How do you choose between your two children? The draconian lockdown rules meant as a family, I couldn't say goodbye to my husband of 37 years and my children couldn't say goodbye to their father. This would have a profound impact upon them. This was the hidden tragedy of lockdown.

Mick's funeral was a simple affair, only 20 could attend, chairs spaced appropriately, social distancing observed, although I could sit with my children. After lockdown, we had a memorial day for family and friends on what would have been Mick's birthday.

Like so many families suffering under the restrictions imposed upon us at times of personal tragedy, when I heard of the 'lockdown parties', enjoyed by those who had masterminded the restrictions, causing such suffering to those who had lost loved ones, I was so angry; what did they know that we didn't? The final insult.

Some months before his death. Mick had complained of pain on his right side, he couldn't sleep on that side. The doctors dimissed this, everything was 'Covid' so a possible underlying condition remained undiagnosed, and Mick passed from Covid pneumonitis, another statistic.

*Alison from Brightlingsea, UK*

Many will have come through the lockdowns unscathed, but for many who suffered loss and still grieve for their loved ones, life goes on. Resilience becomes the watch word, but we will never forget.

**Mick 15.08.1958 - 28.01.2021**

# Brenda

Balance

Balance is the word that came into my head, when I was first thinking of writing this... The whole world has been out of Balance for the last few years and I hope next year we can find Balance.

In my work as a psychic medium, I talk to people every day from every conceivable walk of life, and from all over the world through telephone readings. Astrologically, this has been a challenging year to put it mildly.

Covid and the lockdowns have forced people to reassess their lives, especially relationships and work. Not an easy process, painful but necessary. This has been a difficult year, I have never known so many emotional readings, clients phoning me late at night and early in the morning with fear and worry.

I do feel the second half of 2023 will be better, especially after the Blue Supermoon at the end of August. I believe that the Universe is telling us to press the reset button and move on.

People still have so much fear about Covid even though throughout history viruses come and go - think about how many diseases have been eradicated. Again Balance - Balancing the population.

The mind rules the body, and fear is the most negative emotion, and negativity lowers our immune system.

I chose not to be vaccinated, but I totally respect everybody's individual and personal decision in this, as we all should. However, I am concerned about the number of deaths in 2022 and 2023; above average and in younger age groups, especially in previously fit and healthy people. I cannot believe there is not more publicity about this which is another reason the vaccine disturbs me.

May 2024 be a better year!

# Adriana from New Zealand

A Secondary Science Teacher's Experience of the Vaccine Mandate.

On a warm, muggy afternoon early in January 2020, the skies were a strange opaque orange colour over Auckland city and the sea. The peculiar colour persisted for several days and instilled feelings of eeriness and foreboding. Offsetting these feelings of dread, was the entirely rational explanation that it was because of extensive bushfires rampaging uncontrolled in Australia. The loss of human and animal lives and devastation of the environment was shocking and cause for despair, but the sense of deeper unease the skies created in my heart continued.

At the same time, reports were being broadcast of a deadly virus spreading through China with the potential to kill millions of people. It didn't take long for reports to follow showing the virus had started killing people in Italy and other countries and video footage on the news was terrifying. The deadly virus had been identified as a coronavirus, and the symptoms were similar to flu. Having a background in virology, albeit veterinary virology, I stopped to ponder why this virus, which has long been known to cause flu, was now so deadly. The mere fact that humans across the globe would have been infected with numerous variants of this virus for decades would lead to a huge range of immunity within the global population, meaning that while morbidity with a new variant could be high, mortality should not increase significantly.

Early in 2020, it was still possible to myopically hope that New Zealand would not be affected, but by the end of March massive lockdowns were implemented and normality ended abruptly. On the first day of Level 4 lockdown, I recall locking up the Science Department of the secondary school I was teaching at and telling my HOD that this was a nonsense call made by the government and would only serve to profit Big Pharma. He was alarmed by my cynicism, but I went home and did some research on the World Health Organisation and Centres for Disease Control websites to see what the predicted annual mortality rates were as a result of coronavirus infections. The rates were as I had expected; low but of somewhat greater significance in the elderly and debilitated.

It was challenging for me to understand what was going on, since my own prior knowledge and reading at that point, did not coincide with what we were being told. I had no reference point either, the scale of the unfolding covid drama in the world was enormous, and I felt my own limited insights were insufficient evidence to mount an effective argument. Moreover, there was no one willing to discuss my concerns with me, it seemed I was the only one out of sync with the rest of the world and everyone in my immediate circle.

Teaching remotely through lockdown was a dispiriting and exhausting experience. Being a Science teacher, there are always lots of practical laboratory based experiments, and students generally enjoy the hands-on learning most. I now had to resort to showing videos instead of providing hands-on experiences. It was hard to keep tabs on who was present in the virtual lesson or not and whether they were engaged. Many students experienced home situations where their internet service could not cope with all the occupants needing to be online simultaneously for school or work. Many decided online learning wasn't working for them, occasionally parents discouraged too much screen time. Others may not have had the required hardware and internet connection where they were. Some families were simply too overwhelmed with all the new demands they were facing, thereby placing education low on the priority list.

Staying abreast of student learning was a massive and impossible task. In class it is fairly easy to ascertain how individuals are coping and progressing, but in a virtual classroom, where the student is mostly not visible, bar a name, icon or avatar it is impossible to gauge whether they have logged in and 'disappeared' or are actively engaged. I had to do lots of highspeed learning how to maximise the software we were using to try and include various forms of live interactions. Carefully considered tasks needed to be set, and prudently monitored. The amount of time taken to prepare meaningful short, punchy lessons, to find suitable online alternatives to experiments, to set novel and appropriate tasks, monitor, provide feedback and follow up unfinished work, lack of classroom attendance and so much more, became nearly a 24/7 job.

I threw all my care, energy and enthusiasm into it, hoping that by showing my unfailing motivation and commitment would encourage my students to follow suit. An entirely novel teaching style had to be developed almost overnight and it required continual reflection, re-evaluation and re-designing. It was disheartening to realise that at best, probably fewer than a quarter of my students were managing to stay abreast of their learning.

My days were spent endlessly sitting behind the computer, there was little downtime and none of the collegial staffroom moments and person to person interactions which made school life enjoyable. I missed the daily interactions with kids… well, most of them! Afterall, that is why most people teach. There were opportunities to relate one-on-one via video conference which were rewarding, but was usually student driven, and therefore often involved students who would do well anyway. The significant moments missed were with those who were struggling, and trying to stay under the radar, which they could do very easily online, less so in class.

This is a brief description of my lockdown teaching experience, not just once but four times in Auckland. Living alone added a further challenge of having very little personal interactions with people and this was compounded by criticism I received when my son came to visit from another part of Auckland. It would be fair to add, not all aspects of lockdown were negative, there were moments where, for example, walks to the beach could be squeezed in at unusual times during the day and people found imaginative ways to 'socialise'.

Once back at school, the pressure did not subside, but took on different forms such as catching up student learning missed for various reasons, helping them settle into a routine of hand sanitising, mask wearing, walking specified predesignated routes and managing social distancing in a small classroom space. While this was happening, my school had hired people to constantly circulate and disinfect all touched surfaces. These continual ominous reminders of potential for death were depleting the reserves of teachers and students alike. For me it was a nightmare, since by this stage I had realised that Covid-19 was a planned attack on humanity, but I could not voice my thoughts and could certainly not act on them, forcing me to cajole the vulnerable young people in my care to adhere to the disturbing rituals prescribed, although I became very adept at turning a blind eye!

It went counter to every instinct within me, leaving me reeling in sorrow and frustration. As a mother and a teacher, it is in my nature to nurture, encourage and support youngsters, but I was crippled in the face of their fears, anxiety and questions. An added frustration and a source of loss was being seen amongst most of my colleagues as an anti-vaxxer, tin-hatter and conspiracy theorist and therefore collegiality, friendship and respect were eroded and, in some instances, entirely lost.

Soon older students were starting to ask about vaccination, should they, or shouldn't they? This really compounded my stress. Professionally I could not elaborate my strongly held belief that the mRNA vaccine was a hair's breadth away from genetic engineering (it has now been shown that it is in fact, a gene therapy). With my senior Biology students, who had recently completed a standard on genetic modification, I felt like a fraud for withholding my knowledge from them and tried to subtly guide them to infer this possibility themselves, but I could not step outside of 'professional boundaries' and speak against the school, parents, the government. It was heartbreaking that these were young people with their lives ahead of them, who could be jeopardised so much more than simply losing aspects of their education through lockdowns. They were risking their future health and wellbeing by taking the vaccine! This was a major issue for me, I hold the value of integrity very highly and the deceitful requirement for silence on my part was deeply rupturing.

In October 2021 it was announced that vaccination for teachers would become mandatory by mid-November or face the risk having their careers terminated. A hopeful, optimistic part of me tried to find a way through this madness and I held onto the belief that there would have to be a way around it. After all, don't all problems have solutions if we are creative enough? The resounding answer was 'NO' this problem was insurmountable and at my school termination due to lack of vaccine compliance was a given without any negotiation. There were possibilities for me not to have to lose my job, but the Board of Trustees and Principal were not willing to consider any other alternatives, besides termination.

On Friday 11th November 2021, I was informed by the Principal and Board of Trustees that my role was terminated, and I was not allowed back on site under any circumstances from Tuesday 15th November. If I did venture back onto school grounds, police would be called to remove me. I couldn't believe it, I was still in the process of marking exam scripts and wanted to return them along with verbal feedback to senior students myself, I needed to remove my personal effects and resources from my classroom, return the laptop and keys. More than those mundane tasks was the desire to say goodbye to the many students and staff I had shared much with during my teaching time, but that was not possible either.

The intense shock, sense of betrayal and loss when I was told to go, cannot be described. Up until the Friday, I still held the belief that there was a solution, but by the end of the following Monday, I was forced to leave the school I had poured heart and soul into, a pariah, one not worthy of even a goodbye. I felt stripped to soul nakedness. In the aftermath, a few students, parents and colleagues reached out with kindness and support, and to those I am forever grateful because they returned a sense of humanity to me and gave my soul permission to recover.

Yet I still struggled to accept that the school was completely unwilling to negotiate a way forward with me, one that did not include immediate termination. Surely my contribution, dedication and value as a teacher would shine through and offer some redemption and a way forward? From my perspective, there were definite possibilities which could be explored, and I contacted the teacher's union in this regard. To begin with the union was hesitant to consider my situation since they were supportive of government measures. However, when my complaint was examined, they found that the requirement for fair negotiations had not been fulfilled by the employer and some requests were wrongly refused. Together, we met with the Principal, off site, and my request was that the school reconsider my suggestions, but again was met with a firm refusal. Thus, I lodged a Personal Grievance which was upheld in May 2022 and the school was instructed to pay a compensatory award. The irony is that 15 years prior, the government paid me handsomely to retrain as a Science teacher, and now they were paying me to go away. Bear in mind, all of this was funded by taxpayers.

Once it was clear there was no solution regarding my job, I had to make huge decisions rapidly because I still had a mortgage to pay and no suitable employment opportunities. I decided that I would have to sell my home and find a place anywhere in New Zealand where I could buy and be mortgage free and be able to support myself financially until retirement, a few years ahead.

Auckland was still in lockdown, which meant I could not travel anywhere to find a reasonable home. Ultimately this resulted in many hours spent trawling online real estate pages and Trade Me. My requirements were to be mortgage free and super close to a beach. Lady Luck smiled on me, and I found a delightful old cottage near a wonderful beach and as it was being sold privately by a lady who shared my beliefs about Covid, the house was bought, sight unseen. This may sound idyllic, but there were many stressful hurdles to cross in the buying process while trying to do as much due diligence as I could remotely. Suffice to say, this came with a considerable price tag.

The other side of the buying process was selling my home, which held significant memories and which I had spent many hours decorating, gardening, and improving with pride. It was another defeat to bear, but I sold at the peak of the market which helped to offset the disappointment and enabled me to move on positively from a financial perspective.

Collecting my personal effects and belongings from my classroom also became a nightmare. Where the school had been quite agreeable before I left, this changed afterwards. I had to plead and cajole until finally access was allowed for a few hours just two days prior to my final move to the South Island. It was holiday time, there were no students on site and only a few staff who walked huge rings around me and appeared intent on pretending I did not exist. Fifteen years worth of resources had to be sifted and sorted in those few hours I was allowed, and I shed many tears while clearing up student art, books, photos and my own endless hours of input and years of dedication. All the while knowing there were people on site but not one who passed the time of day; I felt thoroughly rejected and desolate.

In January 2022 I left Auckland, it was sad and exciting simultaneously. Sad because I had lost friends, not only due to leaving but to differences of opinion, lost my cherished home, proximity to my son, my job, income, security and the familiar. I had lived in the same area of Auckland for 22 years. Exciting because I was determined to create a new fulfilling life, filled with activities and time to enjoy so many things I could not fit in around my teaching job. Reframing a negative situation is a helpful strategy to cope with adversity and I was determined to view my move to the South Island as an unexpected and exciting opportunity.

The story doesn't end there of course and it's not as straightforward, but suffice to say, wonderful new people have entered my life, I love my home and the beach, my dog does too! It's been a strange, painful, rewarding, terrifying journey, but one which has aligned me with people who share some of my thoughts, and it's very affirming to know that I am not the only one with concerns in this mad, mad world.

Those ominous orange skies in Auckland early 2020 did indeed portend disturbing times ahead, not only for me, but for all of us in a multitude of ways, regardless of opinions and beliefs held about Covid-19. Sadly, I don't know where this will all lead, I'm not sure it's all over yet despite recent government announcements.

All I can say, is don't take anything or anyone for granted, love your family and friends, live in the moment as much as possible.

## Barbara and Derek Ponsford

So here we are in the middle of the summer of 2023.

It is hard to believe it is a year ago I was sitting writing our story for 'Memories of Lockdown' Book 2. Last year's story seemed so much easier to write than I think this one will be...

We were both hoping that by now, three and a half years later, life would be feeling more like pre-Covid, but to us it doesn't at all; we also talk to many people who feel the same.

During our married life, Derek has always been the one with his glass half full, whereas mine has always been half empty. Now both our glasses are half empty! Only the other morning Derek said sometimes he finds it hard to get up and face the day; what is going to be thrown at us today to worry about...

So, I'll go back to to where I ended our story last year. Following an incident at a local independent market, where a 'Stand In The Park' stall was allocated; the lady who runs the SITP had her stall removed because several Yellow Boards on display with the message 'Would you subject your child to a medical experiment' had caused offence.

As it had been our idea to display the boards, we contacted the organiser to explain and ask if she would reconsider. She wouldn't and she won't reconsider for this year's Market either.

We have displayed our Yellow Boards at several Outreach events in the area instead, with very positive responses, especially from medical and care workers; this same Yellow Board message had completely different positive reactions.

As I mentioned in Book 2, our messages on the Yellow Boards had prompted a 20-year-old man to do some research into the jabs and completely change his mind.

Derek and another guy manned an Outreach table at our own 'Stand In The Park' one Sunday morning, with various information leaflets and the Light paper; a gentleman stopped to chat asking what it was all about so they explained what we are all standing for. He told them that he had had 3 jabs and still got Covid so he wouldn't be having any more. He then told them that he is a Consultant at the local hospital and had seen people die with Covid but not of it, however, he was now seeing many more dying as a result of the jab.

The gentleman shook hands with them both whilst walking off with a 'Light' newspaper and said 'Well done for what you are doing.' It made our day!

We visit other Stand In The Parks where we are always made to feel so welcome - it's such a nice thing to meet other like-minded people for a chat on a Sunday morning. It is also reassuring to see how many more people there are now, people who have done their research over the past years and now think differently.

The Stand In The Parks and the Yellow Boards have been hugely successful, although sometimes it has been a challenge to stand on the side of the road on a rainy cold afternoon in the winter. The awareness we have spread through our messages becomes more and more visible with the amount of 'honks of support' we now get as people drive by and that is very rewarding, and now there are 'Banners on Bridges'.

So getting back to 'what is going to be thrown at us today to worry about'...

Let's start with the NHS, GPs etc. Luckily we haven't needed either but we hear horrific stories from people who have, including my cousin.

He is 72, has diabetes and lives alone. One evening he couldn't move his legs. His phone was out of reach so he had to sit in his chair all night until he managed to attract his neighbour's attention the folowing morning. She couldn't help him. His daughter arrived and called an ambulance. After waiting 5 hours, she called again to be told it could be up to 3 DAYS. I'll repeat that - 3 DAYS!

So with the help of another neighbour they got him into her car and she drove him to hospital. She asked at the reception desk for help and was told there wasn't any help available. She went back to her car in tears and luckily an off-duty paramedic came along and helped her. Unbelievably they then had to wait another 19 hours to be seen. Eventually he was admitted and was diagnosed with the 'flu'. I have never heard of not being able to move your legs as a 'flu' symptom.

I could elaborate more on what followed during his stay, but I feel my blood pressure rising. He did recover eventually. How much faith can we now have in the NHS with stories like this?

Next, the continuing strikes from just about every industry which impact on everyone's lives in one way or another. Is it just us that feels there is something a bit strange, a bit orchestrated about it all?

So to the '15 minute Cities' - now this scares us as much as anything; if people haven't realised what the Lockdowns were really about, they should do by now. In our opinion the Lockdowns were about compliance and now it is about 'control, control, control'.

The other thing that scares us is the thought of a 'Cashless Society' - more and more venues refuse cash. We avoid them all and hand out as many leaflets as possible explaining the reasons why 'Cash is King'.

We felt we were refused a table for lunch one day because we were wearing our 'Cash is King' badges. Although there were tables free we realised that after the lady had noticed our badges, she said there was no availability. Needless to say we won't be going back.

We did have the last laugh at a food show venue when the two ladies in front of us couldn't buy their coffee because when they went to pay by card there was no connection and they didn't have enough cash between them. We felt quite smug when we passed them with our coffees and flashed our badges.

Alarmingly we have heard of bank accounts being closed if you dare to have an opinion that is not in line with the narrative, and also try drawing money out of your account if the amount is a little larger than usual.

We recently read 'The Children's Inquiry' by Liz Cole & Molly Kingsley. 'How the state and society failed the young during the Covid-19 pandemic' It is a very hard read, however we feel that every adult should read this and that this should never happen again

In May 2020 Liz Cole & Molly Kingsley set up a campaign 'Us for Them' to stand up for children's interests during the pandemic and their network of members has since grown into tens of thousands of parents, grandparents, carers and concerned citizens.

Our daughter is a teacher in the Philippines; she has been teaching for many years and has told us this has been the worst year - the impact of lockdowns on the children has been catastrophic.
After being locked up for 2 years, they don't know how to interact with other children which leads to bad behaviour, and children as young as 6 years old needing counselling - heartbreaking!

Moving on to the sadness of the many excess deaths since the rollout of the jabs. This seems to be another big cover up. Why is no one talking about it? If they do, they are shut down immediately.

Where is Chris Whitty now with his 'next slides please?'.
The deaths and the cover-ups are not only happening here in the UK but all over the world. We keep hearing about people dying in their sleep - young people and people in their forties and fifties; the number of people being diagnosed with blood disorders, accelerated cancer and heart problems - when will people join the dots?

Thankfully there are thousands of experts out there who have put their careers on the line to try and get the truth out.
We both enjoyed reading 'A State of Fear' by Laura Dodsworth. 'How the UK government weaponised fear during the Covid-19 pandemic.' How right was she, now we know about Matt

Hancock's whatsapp messages, one of which being: 'When do we release the next variant to scare the pants off them?' - evil man.

In 2018 we had our first visit to 'Parga' on mainland Greece. We loved it and I dreamed of going back but with what has happened the last 3 years I didn't think it would happen - but it has!
We have recently been back for a two week holiday - we had a lovely time and it almost seemed the same as 2018. I say almost, as in the hotel where we were staying we became very friendly with the receptionists and during our stay we heard their stories of the Covid years. They were hard to listen to.

One whose mum and dad are now both vaccine injured and need constant help and another who was forced to have the jab so she could continue her winter job working with special needs children; her boyfriend cried when he was forced to have the jab to keep his job as a chef. She was very emotional when she told us her parents were told by their Doctor that if they refused to have the jab they wouldn't get any more medical care. How wicked is that.

The receptionists also told us that things were exactly the same in Greece as they were back in the UK. Many elderly passed away with very little care and they believed many could have been saved with the correct treatments. In 2020/2021 Covid was recorded on virtually all death certificates. Now, 2 years after the rollout of the jabs, the excess deaths in all age groups are not being recorded as 'jab-related'.

'A very emotional and sad moment - raising a glass of red wine to our dear friends - she had been one of our bridesmaids; it was the day of her funeral and we missed it being in Greece, and 2 days prior to her funeral, her husband passed away too - utterly heartbreaking.'

If we had had any doubts about whether we were following the correct path, this confirmed it.

We also met up with a lady we had met in 2018 in our favourite coffee shop; it was lovely to see her and she remembered us and gave us big hugs. I'm so in awe of this lady. She runs the café with her husband and son, she works 7 days a week from 8am until 11.30pm, going home for just a 2 hour break in the middle of the day. She has done this for two and a half years without a day off and still she greets everyone with a smile. She didn't say much about the last 3 years - only that Covid was like living in a horror movie for them. Hence the long hours she works now to help them survive.

We hear there is another new 'variant'. Just this morning the discussions on the news were about whether we should consider wearing masks again. A Doctor saying we must all go and get our flu jabs and our Covid boosters to keep healthy.

After listening to an interview on UK Column News yesterday between Alex Thompson and Doctor Jobst Landgrebe - that would be the last thing we would be considering. Listening to their scientific knowledge was a very good insight as to just how dangerous this could be and has been... an interview we would advise everyone to hear and then decide what's best for them and their loved ones. It was broadcast on August 17th at 1pm.

There are very many good interviews on UK Column News that you would never hear on the mainstream news broadcasts.

When we first joined 'Stand In The Park' many of the people we met had been watching what was going on unfold over many years and told us that the next 'thing' would be climate change and how right were they. It is constant wherever you look - NET ZERO - NET ZERO - NET ZERO. Many of those shouting the loudest, are the ones helping to cause it - jetting around the world.

The 'Forest Fires' around the world - mostly all at the same time ... quite a coincidence we think. The latest is a fire in Maui and the first book on the Maui fires was published and available on Amazon within a couple of days... Hmmmmm!

We have just watched a video about this book and the fire - all very odd - very hard not to be completely puzzled as to how some areas are burnt and some are untouched.

We also understand there had been talk of turning this area into a 'Smart City'.

Moving on to a happier event - on August 8th Derek turned 80. With our family the other side off the world, I decided it would be nice to have a celebration on Sunday 6th August with all our 'Stand In The Park' friends. We were lucky to have good weather and more than 36 wonderful warriors joined us to celebrate, some from other Stands and areas. We were a bit overwhelmed and felt surrounded by love. I had a birthday cake made, iced with Derek's favourite football team's logo 'Play up Pompey' He took a lot of stick with 'Someone has to support them' - he took it well!

So what have we learnt over the last three and a half years? How naive we have been for a lot of our lives. We had no idea of the depth of corruption across the world. The child trafficking which breaks our hearts. Chem trails across our skies most days. It seems endless.

We know we shouldn't keep looking back but sometimes we can't help it. Our times growing up, our early married life in the sixties when you wouldn't worry if you had forgotten to lock your door when you went out. Times when your next door neighbour would take your washing in if it rained. Mrs Smith would always be there for Mrs Jones. Our children could be out all day and we wouldn't worry.

The same tradesmen called at our homes. The postman would pick up a prescription for you. The Doctor had known you and your family for years, and if you needed him, he or a colleague would be with you as soon as possible.

We think of this and it really hurts - at this moment in time it is all lost!

Our spiritual friends tell us it will all come good and there are wonderful times ahead - we do so want to believe them. We will stay strong and keep fighting.

# Michelle

*The journey continues*
*For our golden boy Boo,*
*Part of an academy now*
*Lots of new training to do.*

*He's steadily working*
*Through levels of support,*
*Reaching each new goal*
*Maya's trusted escort.*

*As an ADIT*
*He must learn at least three tasks,*
*To mitigate Maya's needs*
*React when she asks.*

*Michelle*

*To help with crowd control
Block both front and behind,
When seated, snuggle under her legs
Safety and reassurance she'll find.*

*Deep pressure therapy
He's learning to react,
Using his body weight
To support during a tic attack.*

*Boo's perfecting his job
Settling into his role,
He's navigating the world
Through exercise and control.*

*He has such special qualities
None can compare,
High standards of purpose
Our beautiful Boo Bear.*

*With love and thanks to everyone who has supported Team Boo.*

**For continued guidance from Adolescent Dogs, Assistance Dog Academy and 1-2-1 assistance dog training with Louise.**
**www.adolescentdogs.com**
**www.southcoastdogtrainingschool.co.uk**

# Susan McKinley from Northern Ireland

Like tin soldiers we marched...

My name is Susan, aged 72. I live in Bangor, a picturesque coastal area in N. Ireland. I moved here in 2019 after retirement to be close to my daughter who has lived here for some time. I just loved my new life here, but naturally when lockdown was introduced in March 2020, everything got completely turned upside down.

Now 3 years on, I feel it's massively important that history must never be allowed to forget how broad emergency power and control systems like never before were forced upon humanity at a global level and all in the name of safety and saving lives; and furthermore, as duly decided upon by those self-elected 'health advisors' demanding the right to have the only expert opinions worth considering. It's also now clear that once these freedoms were taken from us, albeit supposedly for 3 weeks as we were initially told, the real intention was to take control over all our rights and freedoms for as long as possible.

Regardless of our different beliefs surrounding a life-threatening global pandemic which led to such harsh lockdown measures, it's possibly or even probably true that most people would agree today that the whole lockdown agenda should never have happened. It's now evident across the world that this extreme response has caused utter devastation, hardship, disadvantage, poverty, ill health, suicides, isolation and so much more for every level within societies, irrespective of where you live.

Looking back to my first memories of lockdown (a term used in the prison service) locally, it all seems like a horrible nightmare. I think to myself, 'Surely that madness couldn't really have happened?' However, it most certainly did and I'd like to tell you my own honest and heartfelt story from the lockdown years and share with you how it all affected my life.

The term lockdown when used by the then Prime Minister, Boris Johnson in his formal address to the nation that this would be put in place, definitely indicated a form of imprisonment to me. I felt incensed by the suggestion that all over 70 year olds must remain in their homes and have younger members of their families leave provisions outside their front doors.

Prior to this I had been enjoying my new long awaited sense of real freedom and spent many happy hours jumping on trains using my free travel pass and discovering new places to visit. I decided straight away, scary virus or not, I wasn't ever going to consent to that self-isolating lark! I lived in a small flat with no garden and I knew I'd go mad if I was to be housebound. Amid the fear, I felt very angry at being told I must stay indoors. I was willing to agree to only going out twice a day for shopping and exercise. I could still enjoy the wonderful walks that I'd discovered which were in reasonable walking distance from my home. I could make the most of these while the weather was good and surround myself with the beauty and harmony of nature, even if everyone suddenly starts jumping out of my way!

As we were forbidden to visit other households, sadly, I had to resign myself to the fact that I couldn't see my daughter for 3 weeks and told myself I'd somehow manage that. We both cried on Mothers Day when we were told these lockdown restrictions would soon begin.

Generally, being trusting and law abiding by nature, I, like everyone else at the time continued to feel scared. These were unprecedented times after all! This all had to be happening for a good reason I thought, and although from past experience, a substantial degree of government incompetence was expected, I believed that actions taken by those holding the power were ultimately about protection. As we all began to adjust to the new, but as we hoped, temporary restricted lifestyles, it seemed essential to tune into the daily government pandemic briefings on TV.

From very early on though I picked up on the deeply dramatic and negative language that was being used by Boris Johnson and his 'health advisors' standing behind their podiums, draped with all manner of psychologically charged visual images and quotes to stir up our emotions - 'Stay Home: Stay Safe: Save Lives' etc... To me their 'science model' just resembled a few weird looking graphs predicting vast numbers of expected deaths from the virus within the UK and around the world. I know I'm no academic but I thought to myself, 'How is this science'? Yes, I thought these guys could talk a good job but how had they calculated these predictions? All seemed a bit suspect to me! I began to notice too that every half hour TV and radio bulletins were giving updates on how these scary numbers were constantly rising.

It soon began to dawn on me that this was scaremongering propaganda at its worst. This together with news programmes repeatedly showing people dying horrible deaths in hospitals around the world, was enough for me to quit watching anything on mainstream news anymore. I found it hard to comprehend the stark contrast between what the TV was telling me and what I saw around my own environment. If this virus was so deadly then why weren't people dying in the streets if they dared to come out of their houses? Also, very shocking to me was the speed that everything got shut down. What remained open - food shops and chemists - was very quickly equipped with perspex screens at the counter to shield the staff from our dangerous presence, and posters telling us to obey social distancing rules were literally everywhere. The sceptic in me thought it rather suspicious that all this equipment was so readily available, almost as if the whole thing had been planned...

Travelling on buses and trains was also only allowed for essential journeys, so that put an end to my regular excursions which helped to fill my days in very positive ways. The queuing to get into supermarkets with only a few people at a time allowed inside seemed the next mad thing to me. I'm sure we all remember when the big red circles placed at 2 metres apart appeared outside to ensure you were social distancing which generally meant queues gathering of nearly a mile long. The rebel in me would never stand directly on a circle but just outside of it. Once inside and only shopping on your own, you had to follow the big arrows around the store and most definitely not turn back again or walk up an aisle the wrong way and get too close to someone... 2 metres apart of course and wear a face mask (anagram of fake scam) if possible.

Shopping became very stressful and a huge challenge, but I enjoyed being brave and walked the wrong way as often as I dared! This felt like living in a clown planet to me and not the world I'd want for myself... talk about being treated like children! Is this what controlling forces want to reduce us to I thought... marching round the supermarket like little tin soldiers with no minds of our own! Perhaps as close to turning us into robots as possible would suit their agenda nicely? When I discussed this mad behaviour with my daughter, she told me she'd been watching a few videos that explained how this was actually to get us to collectively take part in mass rituals. Within unseen human energy fields and vibrational levels which surround us all individually, we can only feel a meaningful connection with others at distances of less than 2 metres. The wearing of the mask symbolizes a loss of right to have a voice of your own. These 2 aspects together symbolize your willingness to be enslaved to the globalist masters who want to break your spirit? This actually made more sense to me compared to the notion that restricting and controlling the movement of shoppers would in any way save lives.

To me there was something deeply suspicious about the news reporting, especially when all media channels around the world were reading from the same script, so who was providing the script? A pandemic of fear was taking hold right across the world - a form of mass hysteria! I believed that deep mind control tactics were being used on the public to scare and confuse everyone and shut down their ability to think logically or critically, and therefore, as I saw it, to have them comply with all the rules, even if they would not necessarily make any sense. I wondered how I could see all this if others couldn't. I have always been empathic and a deep thinker and view myself as fairly intuitive. I've always felt different to others in some ways and didn't quite fit in a lot of the time but it was a shock to me to think I was that different. On reflection though, I knew that over my lifetime part of my learning had been to recognise and free myself from the manipulating and controlling behaviours of parents and others who came into my life. Also, my NLP (Neuro Linguistic Programming) qualification gave me some insights into how people can be hypnotised and programmed without them necessarily knowing it. I reckoned the best of the best behavioural scientists, hypnotists and psychologists were most likely employed (those without a conscience) with the specific aim of formulating a compliant enough nation who'd consent to the extreme new rules government ministers were getting passed, while they kept everyone distracted.

I decided I'd spend my time and energy more constructively and not play into the drama as much as possible - be an observer from a curious perspective rather than a willing participant in a world that had lost all sense of reality.

I had no one other than my daughter to talk to and we supported each other every day. She was on a career break so like me had the time to investigate other sources of information to be accessed online. This opened up a complete re-education for me and once immersed in it there was no going back. Weirdly, this became an empowering activity and information I was uncovering, whilst fascinating was deeply shocking. With my daughter's guidance my search for truth and reason led me to watching interviews and independent news/information channels on YouTube. I watched reports and interviews featuring eminent doctors, scientists, researchers, virologists, immunologists, statisticians etc, all pointing out many falsehoods and distortions surrounding the virus narrative and measures being taken. I noticed how quickly those who had the courage to speak out were threatened and smeared for daring to go against the official narrative.

So, what did I learn? Here's a brief summary - what began in 2020 was to kick off a meticulously planned war on the minds and spirit of the global population. Planned over many decades and influenced through gradual infiltration within governments, institutions and corporations the world's population will be forced into a new global Great Reset and of course not for our best interests. To achieve this the goal is to constantly create enough world disasters so that all economies and monetary systems will completely crash.

Our only survival then will be to let the State look after us in every aspect of our lives. We will own nothing and be happy they tell us (they, being given titles like The Deep State, Cabal and Illuminati).

Contrary to all of this, I've watched many other videos and read some books that promote a Great Awakening where enough of us will join forces on a deeply spiritual level, knowing that we're the ones who have the greatest power. With God/Source/Universe on our side we will defeat the dark forces and prevent them from pushing their totalitarian ideologies onto us. We will win in the end is the message I've heard from so many sources, a peaceful rebellion is taking place they say. This is the message I choose to believe in, no matter how long it takes!

Also, I learned how we've been lied to and stolen from throughout our lives. I discovered how the banking and legal systems were set up to trick us and trap us at every turn. Each have their own language where words that are common to us have a totally different meaning in their worlds. Words are literally used to cast spells on us, hence the word spelling - unbelievably clever but utterly devious and fraudulent!

The weeks and months went by and nothing much changed. Social media platforms like Facebook became flooded with hateful dialogue between those holding different viewpoints. Hurtful and abusive name calling became the norm, all encouraged by mainstream media! The dictatorship tactics of 'divide and conquer' and punish the non-compliant ones was working well! I realised that people with my views were the declared enemy... the 'nut job conspiracy theorists'. I began to feel even more alienated from the rest of the world and afraid to have conversations with people. I felt more secure in my own company and spent many hours on my walks along the seafront. I would often sit on a bench in my favourite spot and have a good cry to myself as nothing around me was making sense anymore. I'd always go to the same bench as on it was placed a brass plaque in loving memory of a lady who had quite recently died. The plaque gave her name and mentioned her joy in looking out into ocean. I would talk to her and tell her how I also found it so peaceful and relaxing, taking in the sea air and listening to the waves crashing against the rocks. I told her I hoped she was happy where she was and that she was better off there as it's too mad down here now!

More of my courage was needed when face masks became mandatory here during the height of the summer months. I just couldn't go along with the mass compliance and declared myself exempt. At first it was really scary going into the supermarket without a mask. I hovered about outside the shop for ages to see if any other brave souls were willing to take the risk. Then I saw a lady who looked older than me walk into the store without a mask so I followed her, I thought, 'If she can do it, so can I'. Even though the experience took a lot out of me, I felt very proud of myself. I promised myself that no one would ever take away my freedom. I remember writing a very stern letter to the manager of a local chemist shop which continued to display a huge poster saying 'Stay at Home: Save Lives' long after this had been mandated. I told him how insulting this was to anyone living on their own and suggested he might use a little more empathy. Thankfully the notice disappeared after a few days.

Then winter took hold and we hoped for normality to have returned by Christmas - no chance of that though! Strict lockdown measures were resumed whilst, as we now know, staff at Downing Street enjoyed their Christmas parties! While they drank their wine together and mocked us, we couldn't spend time with our loves ones or visit elderly relatives in nursing homes! Then came the vaccination rollout. Media and celebrities all pushed the same message... people refusing the 'cure' were selfish granny killers to be cast adrift from society. This placed me deeper into the enemy camp for not agreeing to an experimental and insufficiently trialled new form of treatment, and by this stage I was starting to feel very weary, insecure and isolated.

So where are we now in 2023? Much disclosure is surfacing which for some may be devastating! Many battles have been won but more are emerging to take away our rights and freedoms. It's surely a myth that life has returned to normal now that lockdown measures have ceased. I think all of us have been deeply traumatised over the last 3 years, irrespective of our circumstances. I have felt like giving up on many occasions but something keeps bringing me back and so far, I've not lost hope for a better future.

My heart goes out to young children, as I think much of what they've been subjected to is nothing short of child abuse! Elderly people in nursing homes have also been treated disgracefully and it's good to see that official enquiries and lawsuits against governments across the world are now gaining momentum.

Reflecting on my own spiritual growth and development has been my saviour over these challenging times. My belief that we are all unique, creative spiritual beings having a human existence with infinite connection to an all-powerful higher intelligence has given me strength. What is wonderful to see is a growing number of spiritually aware people coming together to collectively reclaim the power and wisdom that was stolen from us... to know ourselves and help others reconnect to all that is pure and loving. The sharing of heart centred pure love helps to eradicate fear. It bonds us together in a common goal to destroy those who have committed themselves to promoting so much fear in our world. To prevent this from happening, no effort has been spared to divide us through cunningly using identity politics agendas in order to incite more conflict and hatred between us.

I believe though, when enough of us can see, then the show's over! In time we will win!

*'Ballyholme Beach near to where I live and where I would have regularly taken my walks during lockdown'*

# *Holly*

In all the years pre-2020 I was asleep. Asleep to the world and asleep to my own self. My life was focused on moving towards goals constructed by my ego. Buy a house, secure a career, raise children and get married. That isn't to say I wasn't happy because I was. After all, they say that ignorance is bliss and this is true in my experience.

In 2020 the pandemic changed everything. I went through an awakening. First I woke to the world around me and then I woke up to myself. The past 3 years have been a journey of self discovery and all that remains of those carefully laid foundations is my love for my husband and my children.

In 2020 my eyes had suddenly been opened to a world I had never seen before. This world was full of injustice and corruption.

*Holly*

Like a newborn baby, I tried to make sense of my surroundings because here I was in my thirties with absolutely no clue what was happening anymore. I began to question everything I had ever known. No stone was left unturned. Politics, religion, social constructs and history were all under the microscope.

If I have been lied to about Covid, what else have I been lied to about? I asked myself. Once I was aware of the inconsistencies, the untruths and the outright lies, it was all I could see and now that I believed my history to be based on lies, the bottom of my world had fallen out.

I felt that I landed on an island. Alone, scared, destitute and oh so lost. If I looked hard or listened closely enough, I could sometimes make out my loved ones across the ocean on the mainland. There would be moments when the wind would stop howling, the seas would calm and I could see them, I could hear them but I couldn't reach them. The pain was immense. Suddenly I had nothing in common with them anymore. They didn't understand me and I didn't understand them. Our worlds were polarised. Me on a barren wasteland of an island and them, together on the land they believed they had always known. Steeped in history, tradition and heritage. A heritage I no longer identified with. I no longer fit. I felt like I'd lost everything.

Others were following a pandemic closely but I was looking at a much bigger picture. If history had been based on lies, if the version I knew was just a version that fitted the narrative at that time, then who the hell were we? I thought back to my interest in the world wars. A subject I shared with my grandfather. Suddenly my memories felt tarnished. I felt robbed, but mostly I felt sadness. I wanted to go back and close my eyes. I didn't want to see any of this anymore, however even then I knew that was impossible. The only cure was amnesia surely?

So like a resourceful human, as humans often are, I began to devise another plan. Excitement grew as the plan came together and once the plan was made I decided it was foolproof. All I had to do was wake everyone else up. Help them to see what I had seen because once they see the darkness, lies, corruption and injustice they will come over to my island and join me. I wouldn't be alone anymore.

So that was what I set about doing. Building a bridge from my island to theirs by finding information I could share to wake them all up. Hours were spent down rabbit holes digging for the key piece of evidence that was undeniable. Occasionally I thought I'd found it. My heart would race in anticipation. Here it was. The evidence that was undisputable. Tomorrow it will be all over mainstream media and I'll be free from this prison of loneliness and fear. In my head I planned the party. In my mind I heard the apologies from friends who doubted me. I will accept those apologies graciously I decided. There will be no I told you so's from me.

I will accept with compassion and empathy because they have been duped and this isn't entirely their fault either. The system has been clever at trapping people through fear and manipulation, so I will accept those apologies with grace and humility.

The moment never came. No evidence reached the media that would vindicate me and I remained trapped on my island. I realised that my quest for evidence was hurting me. It was making me miserable, keeping me in darkness and dragging me down. I wondered what the point of all this was. I sensed that I had woken for a reason but I just couldn't find the answers. There on my little island, I stalked angrily along the water's edge, kicking up the sand and shouting over the wind to the mainland. Why can't you see what I see? I screamed into the wind. There never came a reply and so my anger and resentment grew.

*Holly*

One night I quite literally looked to the full moon for answers. As I stared at the full moon in all its beauty, I was filled with a sense that I was on the right path. Keep going as you are, my heart said. There is purpose to this journey yet to be discovered. No longer able to seek comfort from others and totally alone on my island, I took great comfort from that interaction with the moon.

I began to scale back my hunt for the elusive treasure trove of evidence. I had no choice really. I was worn out and felt defeated. I realised if I was to survive alone on this island then I needed to rethink how I used my energy. So instead I started to reflect on what brought me to this little island of awakening. It was clear that it hadn't happened to many of my loved ones, so why me? What purpose did this serve in the greater scheme of things? I had no hand in politics.

People were determined to close their eyes to the mountain of documentation highlighting the wrongness of lockdowns and vaccine mandates. No one is going to listen to little old me.

So far, all it had done was ruin things. I no longer wanted to be a nurse. The only career I'd ever envisioned for myself. I didn't give a damn about what door handles needed buying for the new house. I was no longer motivated by saving for the next package holiday abroad. I didn't give a shit about going back to the book club between lockdowns. I couldn't tolerate all the rules. Stay outdoors, stay 6 feet apart, wear a mask, do a test before coming. I was angry because all this awakening had done was create disconnection and dissatisfaction where there once was none. On and on I raged. I was as angry and enraged as the stretch of water that kept me from the mainland.

Then the universe provided me with a miracle. A dear friend returned to my life and landed right on my island. It was like she didn't even need to cross a bridge. She dropped right from the sky and landed next to me on my desolate excuse for a beach.

She had been away for many years on a spiritual journey and as she stood before me talking about her experiences, the hairs on my arms stood on end. Her words spoke to me because I resonated with what she was saying.

My experiences since 2020 have been spiritual, I thought to myself. I just didn't have the language for it at that point. She spoke with such heart and authenticity that she was able to start giving me the tools to start building my own bridges. I finally began to see that my awakening hadn't been about the world around me, it had been about myself. In that moment I was able to let go of a lot of pain and anger and when I realised that I had no part to play in waking up the world around me, I began to feel free.

I realised through speaking to my friend and following her lead that I had been going through a spiritual awakening. An awakening is a process of discovery and this is what I'd been going through on my island. On my hands and knees at the water's edge, I had been sifting through the sand that was my life. My identity, beliefs, morals and principles had been buried there. As I dug around in the sand, I considered which pieces still belonged. With a fist raised before me, I would watch as grains of what no longer served me fell between my fingers.

Putting aside my connection to others for a moment, I began to instead create a connection to myself. I realised that it had been my inner guide that had brought me to this place. It was her that had kept me going forward on this journey even though it caused me such pain. There was always a sense that I was doing the right thing and now I recognised that sense was her. My inner guide. So through breathwork, meditation, being in nature and following the cycle of the moon I began to connect to my inner wisdom. Slowly but surely without even realising it, I began to build a bridge between my island and the mainland. I was less angry, more forgiving and more understanding of other people's journeys. Now I could see what an impossible task I created for myself all those months ago on my island. A person could not wake another person up. An awakening is a deeply personal and autonomous process. It was liberating. I was free and I was finally making my way back to the mainland with the parts of my life that still fit and casting free the parts that didn't.

Once I was more in tune with my inner guide, she came knocking regularly. I began to recognise key themes that had been presented since 2020. Authenticity was one of them. This journey felt like an endeavour to find my authentic self. The self that was hidden behind the ego constructed walls. My inner guide shouted the loudest when it came to my drinking. I had been trying to get sober since January 2020. My sobriety journey predated the pandemic by a mere few months.

Since 2020 I had periods of sobriety but struggled to maintain it. In the end I gave up on giving up alcohol. I'm destined to a life of drinking, I said to myself. This is a part of me I don't think I can escape. However in the early hours of the morning, usually at 4am, I would wake with a thumping heart. My mouth as dry as sandpaper, I would gulp back a pint of water in one go. My heart would hammer in my chest like a bird trapped in a chimney and my mind would race. Often I had no memory of the night before and in the darkness of the night, I would search the darkness of my mind for any clue of how or when I got to bed. Inside my soul was breaking. Why do you keep doing this?, I would berate myself. This has to be the last time, the pleas would then come.

In the daytime when I was sober I would ask myself how my drinking aligned with my authentic self. The answer was it didn't. Alcohol prevented me from addressing my other key theme, connection. I couldn't connect to myself when I was drinking. I couldn't connect with my values, purpose or goals. Like every grain of sand before it, alcohol was now under the microscope and it wasn't looking good. I finally realised that it was my inner guide waking me up at 4am.

My soul was shouting so loud it was rousing me from sleep. Drawing parallels from the beginning of 2020, when I saw it, I couldn't unsee it and I began to move towards freedom. I reflected on how well my inner guide had led me until this point and I was going to continue listening to her. I've now been free from alcohol for many months and I think this time the change has stuck. It's amazing how many other doors have opened to me now I'm no longer shackled by a desire to drink. Hangover free, I do the things that create inner connection naturally. I'm out in nature more, I exercise, I eat better, I write and I'm happier. I dance in the kitchen and sing loudly when I'm in the car. Where there was once anger, my heart is now filled with joy and I have my journey in finding myself to thank for that.

My connection with others is more of a work in progress. It's taken me a long time to start figuring out this new me. There are some friendship circles where this new me doesn't really fit anymore. To tell you the truth, if I told most of my old circle that I had gone through a spiritual awakening they'd look at me like I'd grown another head.

Getting sober has impacted on a few relationships as well. However I no longer feel lonely, scared or angry. I don't look at these old relationships and feel anger that those people couldn't meet me on my journey. This is my journey not theirs. I have found myself in the process and that feels far more valuable.

Standing here in 2023, I'm so very grateful these last few years have happened. If it weren't for the pandemic, I would still be asleep and I find that difficult to think about. The truth might hurt but it's still the truth and once you know the truth you can set about learning how to deal with it.

*Holly*

In the spirit of authenticity, I have a confession. In my last chapter in book 2, I signed my name as Samantha. I used a pseudonym because at the time I felt under great pressure working within the NHS. I'd been so scrutinised by my choice not to take the vaccine that I didn't feel brave enough to sign with my real name. I regret that now and it doesn't fit with the new more authentic me.

So my name is Holly. Thank you for taking the time to read my story and thank you to dear Rosanne for giving me the space to tell it.

If anyone has been left wondering what happened to my career in the NHS, well I'm still in it. I'm still working in the same assessment role that I detailed in book 2. My plans to leave are more certain now. I don't know exactly what that looks like at the moment, however I have plans for courses next year.

My role in the NHS was one of the very first grains of sand that I looked at and realised no longer served me, however I never really was on my own little island. I was in a semi-detached house with a mortgage and children to feed so I have had to make the NHS work for me until I can finally let it slip through my fingers to join the rest of the debris of my pre-2020 life.

# Monica

A Beautiful Connection.

The roots of my experiences of the last three years or so involved a very powerful vision of the future received thirty-three years ago.

I had always had a connection with the realms beyond the physical since an early, very significant spiritual experience. As a child it was normal for me to feel a strong sense of foreboding that foretold a potential negative situation. Inexplicably I could sense lies, smell an impending robbery or even smell when someone was going to die. Fortunately, that didn't happen often, I hasten to add.

I was 25 when, during a deep meditation, I was advised of a time to come. I was alone, but I distinctly heard a male voice say

"You will enter a time of chaos on Earth and you will need to help your family." Sensing the enormity of this responsibility on my little shoulders, I immediately mentally replied "They will never listen to me."

Meanwhile, as if looking out through a living room window, I was being made aware of the future whilst simultaneously being told "You will have to find a way."

The future did indeed seem truly chaotic. Scenes of a revolution taking place on our streets were filled with people looking angry, almost completely disorientated. Most were shocked and confused, whilst others seized this as an opportunity to senselessly kill out of rage. The level of uprising was unprecedented. Directly up above the scene on the streets, I was being made aware that some of the populace were leaving the planet. I was overcome by the sensation that it would not be everyone.

Time flew by quite quickly after this vision. With no incidents requiring an evacuation from Earth, I continued life as normal until the 19th of August 2019 when, mysteriously, I began to hear a Michael Jackson song playing in my head. I really did not care for the song too much but it was relentless. 'Heal the World' nagged and nagged at me for days until one desperate, sleepless night, at precisely 2.38 in the morning, I woke up to search for the lyrics. I was astonished. Words that I had never paid attention to before, suddenly began to infuse new meaning into my being. I was receiving a message as clear as day, well, night in this case, and I needed to pay attention.

Observing that I was in clear communication, I made a point of asking who I was in speaking to.
"Who are you? Are you GOD?"
"Yes" the answer came.
"No, No, No, No, Nooooo. People will never believe me if I say

that" I exclaimed. I was overwhelmed, bordering on a state of shock to say the least.

"If it is you," I said bravely, "I need a sign." I didn't know what sign but requested that something appear to prove who I was speaking to.

The next morning, whilst talking to someone on the phone, a loud burst of music began to play in the street below the flat where I lived. I knew from the usual hustle and bustle of the day that most people were either at work or at school. Looking down onto the street there was no one, but there also seemed to be no indication of where this music was coming from either. Everything seemed normal. I fixed my gaze on a workshop below thinking that this had to be where it was coming from. My suspicions soon proved wrong when the men working there closed up shop and left. The music continued booming nonstop.

Sensing no hope of truly discovering what was going on, for some reason, I began to pay closer attention to the music. It dawned on me that I was hearing Michael Jackson songs playing nonstop, one after the other. I asked the caller who was still on the phone whether they could hear it too. Thankfully they could. It was not just in my head.

We hung up the call but I remained perplexed. This music continued for another forty-five minutes with no radio announcements or interruptions. Then, I remembered having asked for a sign the night before. Defeated by my disbelief, I sat on my bed and said, "OK, I believe." Within milliseconds, the music stopped. It sounded like the screech of a needle on a vinyl record. Still in disbelief I incoherently, but jokingly, said, "You can really do all that stuff with the music, and electromagnetics can't you?"

"Yes, the answer came."

Slowly acquiescing, I asked, "Now that you have my attention, what do I do?" I heard nothing. There was no answer.

Three days later again at 2.38 in the morning, I was woken up once more to the sound of Michael Jackson. This time the song 'Let me show you' was playing in my head. Again, totally amazed by the lyrics, I knew something was being communicated. "Let me show you the way to go."
"OK!" I said, then went back to bed. As I lay trying to sleep, I remember thinking, "It's OK receiving messages from you but can you choose a more reasonable hour next time?'

Three days later at 11.30 pm, yet another song was playing in my head. 'I'll be there' by The Four Tops. The lyrics seemed to be indicating that, despite everything I had been through and will go through,'I'll be there.' I not only expressed my gratitude that night for receiving this message but also for moving the timing to before my bedtime.

I heard nothing until I was unmistakably asked a distinct question a few months later in October 2019. "Whose side are you on? Man's side or my side?" By this time, knowing who this was, I immediately replied, "Your side. Of course."
"Good," came the response, "for I am asking everyone one by one whose side they are on. For in my Kingdom there are many mansions and you shall want for nothing."
"Oh, OK." I answered innocently. I was not quite sure what all of this meant, being a Buddhist, but somehow, I felt comforted knowing that God had my back too.

Then, in early February of 2020 I began to hear another song. 'Change is Gonna Come' by Sam Cook. I remember listening to different versions of this song, even dancing to some of them, but as there had been a gap in communications with God, I was thinking more about the song rather than the message it had for me.

I don't normally listen to the news, but something began to trickle through into my awareness about happenings in China, some illness or other.

Meanwhile, a friend (whose name just happens to be Janet Jackson) had asked if I could come and spend a short time with her as, not only was her son in bed recovering from a spell in hospital, but she was feeling very anxious. They lived alone so would feel better if there were someone with them just in case. This arrangement would not affect my daily routine so I agreed.

Whilst packing some basic things one night, the song 'Change is Gonna Come' was even stronger and louder in my head. Then came a communication.
"There has been an age-old war between myself and those of less light."
"Why?" I thought.
"They do not have the keys to creation."
"Oh! OK" I said, continuing my packing and not thinking to enquire further.

News about this illness was beginning to take hold in the media and there were reports of it spreading. Feeling a little irritated by this intrusion, my internal lie detector slowly began to come online. I remember thinking here we go again. If it's not this, it's that. If it's not the bird flu, it's the pig flu. If it's not the pig flu, it's the insinuations behind the Spanish flu.

What now! Something was up but I was paying very little attention until I finally moved to my friend's house. Within a few days, we were in the first lockdown. A change had indeed come. During these first two weeks, then another two weeks, then another until June 2020, I can safely say that these were the best two weeks of my life. The world stood still. The tranquillity, peace and quiet was palpable. A beautiful sound of silence not only to my ears but to my entire being.

My memory of this time remains fresh till now. Every morning without fail at around 8am just as I was stirring in bed, I was visited by a bright white light that scanned my whole body then left. It came in through the bedroom window and stayed for what felt like ten to fifteen seconds. I had to remain very still. Not even think, otherwise the light would retreat then disappear. I loved every moment and felt that a profound spiritual connection with humanity was taking place. Many were either too glued to the news, programming, or their personal situations to feel the subtlety of what was taking place.

Looking out into the chaos in the world at that time, I knew that this had everything to do with the vision I had had all those years ago. I also knew it was a message about my wider family too. I have had many communications since then and with a bit more insight can now see the ricochet effect that many years of misguided, individual and collective actions are having not just in every individual life but on the planet too.

'The great clean up' is at hand as we all go through our personal dark night of the soul to understand and repair our inextricable link with nature in preparation for our evolution. These communications have continued to inspire me, not only to create an energized product for emotional stability but also to help earthbound souls to evolve, and various programmes to help others connect to their true purpose for entry into abundance.

"You all are a storehouse of treasures awaiting discovery. The new currency is the heart!"
God.

## Skye Coelho

*"It is not the strongest of the species that survives, not the most intelligent that survives, it is the one that is most adaptable to change."*
**\*Charles Darwin.**

I began writing this from a Travelodge up north in the UK - a long way from my life living in a caravan off grid in southern Spain...

On the plus side, this is a beautiful historic part of the country, and the people up here seem much more open and friendlier than down South (sorry fellow Southerners!).

Welcome to post-pandemic UK 2023.

So how did I arrive here?

From one second to the next, my life changes often beyond recognition, both for better or for worse depending on your vision of life, adventure and adaptability... The ability to adapt and always be grateful for food, a roof and a warm bed helps me to overcome the shock of sudden change; whether it be holed up in a Travelodge in the UK, a caravan in the Spanish mountains, a squat, or a billionaire pad on the palm in Dubai... Yes, I've seen, stayed and lived in all the previous and more. I believe you must live it all to possess true adaptability, understanding of how others live, be grateful and have a wide vision on life... I had converted an old, abandoned caravan, (you read about that adventure in the last book!) and was living completely off grid with one solar panel and no running water until I got the call that I was dreading...

Someone close to me was severely ill with Anorexia Nervosa and needed my help. Within 48 hours I was on a plane with a change of clothes and little else, my only focus on how to help and how I would navigate the crumbling health system and non-stop bureaucracy with barely a dime in my pocket, and with my own mental health a tad in crisis after the last hellish few years of death and trauma. I was hoping I would be strong enough to cope with this enormous emotional strain, the bleak British winter and wherever this journey of anorexia would lead us...

*"Remember, Lexi, that mothers and daughters are made from the same batch of stardust, and when you are sad, I'm sad, and when you are happy my heart sings."*
**\*Amanda Prowse, 'The Food of love'.**

Nineteen hours in an NHS waiting room after waiting nearly 8 hours for an ambulance... I recorded the words of the person I was accompanying and her journey through this experience:

*'Why am I here? I'm not even sick. I've eaten. I'm not anorexic. I'm a fraud. I'm 41 kilos of fat. I'm an imposter. I'm going out of my mind, I hate it here. I'm not sick!*

*I want to cry when I see the elderly man slumped forward in a chair. He's been here even longer than us. Then there's the bright, funny sprightly 89-year-old ex-ballroom dancer who's also been here all day and night in the same chair. She's humorous and lively, we love her but makes me so sad and angry she's here alone in a chair. Where are the beds?*

*Thank God for some of the amazing nurses who keep our spirits high. Our rather loud, camp nurse with his blonde bouffant hair, the cheeky life and soul of the party, is busy organising, caring and serving drinks as if we were at a party. He has a heart of gold and calls everyone 'love'. It feels like another era and I'm momentarily comforted… He and our 89 yr. old, let's call her 'Dill', form an instant connection and the laughter flows even when we are all exhausted in the early hours, and at our lowest ebb...*

*Our small group of stoic sick people form a bond to stay strong and keep going. 2 am. Everyone snoozes at some point except me. I feel horrendous. I go to the machine and binge on some chocolate and nutty bars then make my way to the chapel where I cry, feeling like a loser and the pain in my stomach returns with a vengeance... It's my punishment for eating.*

*A gentleman appears beside me, he looks slightly wary of the sobbing anorexic in a unitard huddling in the chapel but introduces himself and I instantly feel like he's judging me for eating… I slowly open up, crying as I tell him my story. He shares his: Cancer.*

*He has also been sitting in a chair for over 19 hours awaiting chemo and a blood transfusion. He doesn't want to die any time soon; he wants to see his grandchild grow up.*

*I just want to cry and cry it's all so wrong. So unfair. My brain is exploding, I'm claustrophobic. I've been awake 72 hours. I can never rest. I'm on constant alert ready to flee, always on fight or flight mode. I feel so ill but I'm not even sick. They don't understand. I'm in control. No one gets it. I just can't stop crying. They say my blood pressure is low. The convulsions were just because I'm cold.*

*Disassociation, I don't recognize myself in the mirror, all I see is a stranger. I feel like a loser, I fail at everything, I make everyone unhappy, the only thing I've succeeded at is starving myself. I want to be normal like other people, not care what I look like... My OCD is through the roof... but I'm fine... Though staring at a perfectly made bed and unable to lie on it for fear of messing it up is not fun, it's exhausting...*

*We are all hot, exhausted and frustrated. The nurses are doing their best. It's not their fault. There are only two doctors all night for tons of people... I just want to run and breathe... We finally leave the hospital at 3pm the next day... The elderly man still slumped in his chair... Dill waves goodbye, still upbeat and cheerful in the wheelchair and I just want to cry when I see George still waiting in his chair, suffering with his cancer. I don't want him to die..."*

Distressing, very difficult to read, horrendous for the sufferer and their loved ones. From what I initially thought would be a few weeks turned into 5 months. I would never have believed what we went through if I hadn't experienced it first-hand.

From Shropshire to London and on to Brighton, infinite experiences including contacting a Labour MP who endeavoured to intervene and aid with our battle to receive help from the eating disorder services and mental health team. Amidst all this, I managed to complete another book, my memoirs, 'Life's too Short for Ironing' a collection of essays, articles and poetry.

Just after completing my book, the dear friend who housed us in Brighton died suddenly, and then another friend in Spain… Grief has been non-stop the last three years, birth and death being the only real aspects of life that unite all humanity in my humble opinion, I just wish there was more unity and less division in this world…

As I write this back in Spain, I think back to these last months and all the people that crossed my path; So many places, so many people come and gone, but hey, it's what makes life interesting isn't it?

"It's been a long, long ride,
Don't know where I'll sleep tonight.
Oh under the stars
Or maybe in your bed alright.
Against the wind
I crossed your desert today.
Don't care what you say
Cause baby I'm goin'a stay.

Yeah I'll comb this whole beach over
Trying to find the love that'll stay.

It's been a long, long journey
Don't know where I left my mind.

**\*The Allah Lahs. Long Journey.**

## **Overview**

In the first book I made it very clear my views on the pandemic, the way it was handled or better put, orchestrated. In these last three years almost everything I wrote about has come true, and this not a good thing. Is this madness over? Not by far. We shall see more unimaginable changes in society, on the planet and what I can only describe as state  sponsored terrorism against the people. Total collapse of this current order and a whole new era. It will not be an easy ride but these last few years have already been hellish on so many levels, yet simultaneously much beauty has grown through new connections, awakenings and realizations. I hope to survive long enough to see a new world, out of the darkness into the light and a true freedom never experienced by any of us living beings.

"I wish you all peace on this journey and may the force be with you!"

# Mark Watson

Normality has returned to the island of Patmos. Well, an almost version of it. Covid has pretty much gone from daily life. I buzz about on my moped, buy local courgettes, tomatoes and peppers from Petros' farm truck, queue somewhat gratefully in the Post Office air conditioning in the hot July sun, with barely a thought of the disease that constantly held the limelight, front and centre stage, for 2 years.

There are reminders of course: a few light blue masks still flip around in the Meltemi wind in the ditches beside the road, but the fears of the Aegean becoming a Pacific PPE garbage patch haven't materialised. There are the occasional masks worn by the locals – Yiorgio the pharmacist, the nameless DHL lady. These are all sparks, occasional blips if you like, a glimpse of the mountaintops, of something that was once much bigger.

There are other memories too. Of closed winter cafés, of weird handshakes, of no one knowing what 2 metres distance actually was. One in particular: talking to the nurse practitioner in a hospital in Prescott, Arizona when I was having a lung checkup in late 2022. She was on the respiratory ward during Covid.
"Did you see many people die during the disease?" I asked her.
"One day," she said, "everyone on the ward died."
"How many did you see die altogether?"
"Four or five hundred."
"Old, young?"
"All ages."
"Were they in denial?"
"Most realised it was the end when it was."

That still haunts me, but generally thoughts of the disease have been largely back-burnered.

So where does that leave us on the island, post Covid? I'm not too sure. Greece, life on the island, continues, but everyone knows something happened and it's all not quite the same. The 2019 carefree holiday attitude is still there, but it feels different now, not quite as all embracing – everyone knows now that rain clouds can form in our normally sunny Aegean summer skies.

Looking back I still find the conspiracy theorists, the deniers that Covid didn't even exist, tedious. That it was all just mask manufacturers making the whole thing up in order to sell masks, deluded. Having lived in LA a long time, the idea that my own personal angel/spirit guide knows about Zoolan ding dong whatever energy

that comes from the planet Phlarquon and that'll keep me safe, slightly mad. But something solid underneath seems to have emerged from that side of the fence which cannot be denied - and that's that the surveillance world, which was already there and progressing fast before Covid started, took a giant leap forward during the pandemic. The tide has retreated a bit with regard to this, but it's still coming in, and during Covid we all suddenly got to see what has really been going on - and it's not pretty.

Where will this end? I don't know. It could be good, it could be bad, but I still cling to hope for the positive.

Put it this way. I watched the 8 o'clock Sunday morning ferry arrive from Athens 2 days ago. All the usual sights and sounds were there. The trucks hissing and wheezing and jerking to sudden halts as they come off the ship to avoid hitting the tourists pouring off the ferry dragging their suitcases behind them; the port police blowing whistles, shouting, waving cars this way and that, all to absolutely no effect; people with beaming smiles rushing up to hug their arriving loved ones – all the wonderful beautiful chaotic mess of humanity trying to organize something and getting nowhere near it, but it all somehow working.

Such sights give me glimmers of hope for the future. For the greater spirit of mankind. That somehow the threat of 1984, the next pandemic, whatever our future challenges are going to be, we might be more united next time, we might treat each other a bit better, and somehow get there together. How, I don't know. But somehow we have to do better than we did with Covid. All of us. Me included.

As for right now, I'm heading down the hill past the goats standing up on the highest rocks catching the cooling breeze, past Shabby, the old donkey, who we feed our watermelon rinds and cucumber shavings to, past the magenta Bougainvillea cascading over the taverna roof, and I'm going for a swim in the warm clear waters of our bay.

Still feeling privileged. Less so than in 2019 perhaps, but hoping for that brighter future, for the greater spirit of mankind to come through somehow, no matter what.

See you on the other side of the rainbow.

# Veronica

Hello once again!

It's hard to believe it's been over three years since all this madness began. Hard to believe I was 17, and that now I'm 21. It feels like an eternity has passed, and yet also, somehow, no time at all. Time is weird nowadays. The days are incredibly long, but the weeks and months fly by.

My life this year has been both quite similar and quite different to last year. I spent the first five months of the year solely working, before going on a solo trip to Europe for a month and a half, which was full of fantastic experiences. Then I changed my University and course, and am now studying something completely different! All in all, it's been a really, really good year and I'm so very thankful for it.

Anyway... I want to be honest here – I have virtually no hope for a good future. Sounds harsh, but it's true. Life will continue to get worse (and worse and worse and worse), for reasons I won't get into because it's just too much, in terms of explanations and on an emotional level too. I don't see myself living to see my 40s – and that's being extremely optimistic.

So life, now, is simply about having fun and enjoying the time I have. For example, I'm only doing Uni because I'm learning something that's interesting and keeps me busy in the short term, not because it's something that'll turn into a career. I know it never will.

Don't get me wrong, I'm not unhappy. Not at all! I'm really enjoying my day-to-day life. Most of my weeks are great! I try to focus on the little things. And for the most part, I pretend nothing else is going on outside my bubble. Some people will say that's cowardly, but it hurts too much to think about. I still have those days of sadness, those days where it hits me, but I'm able to move on better than I could a year ago, and the days occur further apart. It does get easier to deal with. It gets easier because it has to. Our brains can only cope with so much continuous sadness and anger.

My view on the last three years has not changed. I still stand by pretty much everything I talked about in my last two reflections. Except now I've truly reached the stage of not wanting to talk about it. It hurts too much when I think back on lockdowns, on the mandates, on all the madness the last three years has brought. A part of me still can't believe it all happened.

I wish everybody the best of luck and happiness in the future.
xxx

# Janet Jackson Tyler Lummer

Well, the pandemic is over.

So what have we learned during these 3 years about OURSELVES and OTHERS? What kind of choices did we make during this time? How fearful did we become? Did it all turn out the way you thought it would when it started? Do you still have the same friends? Are you still living in the same place you were in when it started? Did you have family and friends that died during the pandemic? Did your mental state alter during this time? Did you become depressed? Did you lose parts of your memory? Did you lose your job? Did you get a new job? Do you need help?

I am just full of questions at this point, because I believe these are all the questions we should ask ourselves and our people that are in our lives.

I learned that without my belief in God I would have suffered terribly. Man had no concrete answers during this time. The uncertainty in the world was outrageous and confusing and the fear it created killed people. I know my faith in God was what saved me from being depressed and scared. No matter what the news reported and all the opinions on social media, I still had a clear picture of what God has promised me and I held on to that for dear life.

I knew we would come through this and I saw all the teachings of love that were to be learned during this time, if you only could recognize the signs, and start to live in this way. I believe many people started to understand how important the people in their lives were and gave more thought to their relationships during this time, and they also took stock in what made them really happy in life and how they needed to treasure this and protect it.

People also realized that they could have a completely different life and career by starting to work at home and realizing they loved it because they had more time with their family and friends. They could be anywhere in the world and still get their work done, but had never thought of that before the pandemic.

Even though we were made to stay at home during certain timeframes during the pandemic, now we are freer than before in regards to our working schedules. Some wonderful healthy lifestyle changes came because of the pandemic and the lockdown situation. It made us think out of the box and care more for each other.

Our duty and promise to humanity now is to keep these new thoughts and ideas going and continue to think of others ALL the TIME and stay connected to your families as much as possible, and know they are your source of love. Stay grateful for your life and health. Communicate with each other ALL the TIME. The more we question each other about our lives, the more we learn to understand life.

Writing for Rosanne's Trilogy has been a blessing for us all. I have seen that people who do not particularly agree, still can come together and write how they feel, and feel free in doing so. Learning things that were happening in a part of the world that they did not even live in. Everyday people expressing themselves and enjoying hearing the experiences of others. I hope that one day all the people that have written in the Trilogy will be able to come together for a weekend retreat somewhere in the world to talk about our lives with each other.

Thank you Rosanne for your kindness and honesty. You wanted us to express how we were feeling in order to share, in hopes to help someone. I believe you have succeeded and I look forward to sharing on your website many more events in my life and hearing about everyone else's.

God Bless you all and talk to you soon.
Always In Spirit,
Janet Jackson Tyler Lummer

# Anne

Fading Memories.

It's almost exactly two years since I wrote my first piece for Vol 1 of the Memories of Lockdown. I didn't contribute to Vol 2 as I recall I was too busy transitioning back into a 'normal' life again and trying to make my own sense of it all. Now two years later it feels like a good time to take stock and reflect on what we all went through.

By and large for me now, it's like lockdowns never happened. We had a few in Britain, some more difficult than others over 2020 and 2021. Everyday life was disrupted like never before and while I and my family have, I like to think - bounced back to 'the good life' reasonably easily I still feel very concerned about the impact of the lockdowns on children and young people, and how that will manifest over time. It seems we have a cohort of children and young people who fell behind during the pandemic and have not really re-engaged. The latest attendance data from the Department for Education in England revealed that absences in the spring term this year (2023) were still 50% higher than before the pandemic. In Wales where I live, one in five children in Wales are now regularly missing school.

Having worked with, and for vulnerable children and young people most of my life, I understand the evidence that links this kind of disengagement from school to poverty, poor mental health and crime. Absence from school has a profound impact on individual life chances and incurs major costs to society, with absent pupils over-represented in the population leaving school not in education, training or employment (NEET).

The Centre of Social Justice recently published an analysis of the 200,000 pupils projected to leave school in 2025, a cohort it dubs as the 'lost generation' as they began secondary school just as lockdown measures were taking affect.

Responding to the CSJ's report, the Chair of the House of Commons Education Select Committee, Robert Halfon MP pulled no punches: 'Covid-19 has wreaked havoc in our schools. Young people's life chances have been laid to waste by successive school shutdowns and interruptions to their learning. The damage caused by lockdowns could not be clearer than in the case of school attendance: the pandemic has given rise to a generation of ghost children. If we're not careful, we are creating an Oliver Twist generation of children exposed to significant safeguarding hazards including tough domestic situations at home, online harms and joining county line gangs.'

It seems we will all be living with the impact of lockdowns for many years to come. It will take the world a long time to recover…

I remember the pandemic as a scary time – I didn't lose anyone close but I still remember the horror of those pictures on the television from Italy, and then India (in particular) and the dreadful daily announcements of the number of deaths. I do think the caution was justified, I believed and still believe, in the science and I understand the reasons for the lockdowns. But now I'm troubled by the fact that children and young people in the UK, and no doubt across the world, were so disproportionately badly affected, primarily by the closure of schools. Looking around at the way other governments handled the situation illustrates that it needn't have been so draconian. France for example only shut schools down for one period early on in the pandemic (in 2020) and then kept them open.

Lost but not forgotten: the reality of severe absence in schools post-lockdown.

On a personal level I have certainly bounced back to a pretty happy existence. Early in 2022 I decided to finally retire from my day job. I didn't much enjoy conducting research interviews on Zoom or leading training modules from a distance, down a camera rather than in person. Reflecting back on my decision now I can see that Covid and its impact on my work modus operandi was actually the 'kick up the bum' I needed to give it up. I've no regrets and am very much enjoying spending more time with my family and friends, growing veggies on my allotment and going places.

John and I have been able to continue with our sporadic and sometimes extended travels over the last 18 months – we spent much of the northern hemisphere winter this year in Sydney visiting close relatives, we've been to a few music festivals this summer and we are heading off in our camper van to southern Spain in a few days time with no return booked.

In September last year, after 2 years chez Crowley, Bob (the Collie we adopted in the first lockdown) went to live with another family. He lives with Chloe a young autistic woman and her mum. Chloe had recently lost her trusted canine companion and she fell in love with Bob. He's very happy in his new home and is much loved; he even has his own instragram account and I get regular photos and updates.

I am grateful for the vaccine and get boosted whenever I am offered the jab. I have had Covid a couple of times and whilst I wasn't seriously ill, it's not nice and I'd rather avoid it if can.

Of course now my travelling is not affected by Covid restrictions but by the self-inflicted madness of Brexit, which means I can only be in the European Union for 90 out of every 180 days. My husband who's Irish can go wherever he pleases in Europe for however long he wants. I can't and it really pisses me off. For some time the pandemic served as a convenient smokescreen for the disastrous impact of Brexit on Britain's economy and our standing in the world, but now the mists are clearing and it's all coming into sharp perspective. Post-Brexit Britain is most definitely going to hell in a handcart although I'm hopeful necessity will eventually lead to closer ties with Europe, at least as far as trade is concerned.

In terms of the future I'd like to think the world has woken up to the need to co-operate and work together to combat global issues that impact on us all (including dangerous viruses), but I'm not too hopeful right now. During the pandemic it was wonderful to see the co-operation amongst scientists to analyse data and thereby increase our understanding of the virus and how it spread, as well as developing an effective vaccine, but we seem to have reverted to competitive, and even combative, modes again.

I guess the rodeo show in Britain is over with Boris now out of politics and the influence of the Right in the Tory party (temporarily?) somewhat dulled. The new threat to us now (according to the Daily Mail) is 'the small boats' and all those migrants who risk their lives at sea to come to Britain to better themselves. Ironic when these people flee from countries we used to think we owned and we definitely exploited. Doubly ironic when the economists remind us that we have an increasingly large proportion of older people in our population who are not economically active, and we need young workers to come to this country to run our services and pay taxes to fund our pensions and our health and other public services.

It's me and my fellow Baby Boomers - born in the mid-to-late 1940s and the 1950s – contributing to the growth in the numbers of people aged 65 and over (11 million – nearly one in five of the population and rising) and somehow I think we'll be needing a few more youngsters to look after us.

## *Do You Remember?*

masks - hand sanitisers - social distancing - stay alert - support bubble - quarantine - key workers - protect the NHS - working from home - children's playgrounds cordoned off - gyms closed - public toilets closed - touching elbows instead of shaking hands - essential workers - disinfecting shopping bags - 3 weeks to flatten the curve - next slide please - non-essential shops closed - pubs closed - track & trace - cafes closed - libraries closed - schools closed - parents juggled work with home-schooling - arrows painted on pavements & floors to show you which way to walk in stores and on streets - self-isolate - PPE (personal protective equipment) - furlough - strict stay at home 'guidance' - parties at Downing Street - to keep you safe - people only allowed to go out for food, medical supplies and daily exercise - no mixing indoors - hospitality businesses closed - safe and effective - the vaccine will stop you from getting covid - side effects - the vaccine will stop you from passing the virus on - new variant - more lockdowns - police moving people on in parks for sitting on their own on a bench - myocarditis - defibrillator - died suddenly - excess deaths - yellow card system - tier system - new normal and much more ...

The following information on the UK government website:
'As of 19 March 2020 COVID-19 is no longer considered to be a high consequence infectious disease (HCID) in the U.K.'
Didn't the government shut down the country because of a 'high consequence infectious disease?'

Supermarkets - queuing outside as only a certain amount of people were allowed in the store at any time - traffic lights on supermarket doors to indicate when you could go in - constant announcements to stay safe - plastic screens around shop tills

GPs - face-to-face appointments decreased by more than half in April 2020 and some surgeries closed their doors.

Matt Hancock's leaked whatsapp message to his government mates 'what shall we say next to scare the pants off them?' - to ensure compliance with Covid-19 restrictions, while discussing when to "deploy" details of a new strain.

Care Homes - family and friends advised not to visit care homes, except next of kin at end of life. Alternatives to in-person visiting included the use of telephones or video. Plastic or glass barriers between residents and visitors. Relatives watched their loved ones deteriorate from windows, pods and the other side of screens. Our poor elders, many not understanding what on earth was happening and finding themselves alone day after day, many of them until their death.

Carer - a carer looking after several people daily giving care which required close contact, consistently going from one person/house to the next - their families were not allowed to visit at all.

Hospitals - UK hospitals tightened restrictions on visits - even to dying patients. Some hospitals supplied iPads and phones to help visitors say goodbye to loved ones.

Masks - required in shops and anywhere near another person. Some people chose to wear masks while driving alone in their car and some when walking alone in the countryside - some never wore a mask at any time. Some believed that wearing a mask protected them while others thought wearing a mask was like trying to contain a mosquito with a chain link fence. We read that wearing a mask long-term could cause health issues, we also read that masks were effective and safe to wear.

Discrimination against those who chose not to have the 'vaccine/ jab' - labelled as anti-vaxxers and granny-killers
Daily under threat from voices on the TV including Piers Morgan who called those who chose not to have the vaccine (for many different reasons) 'selfish pricks who should be thrown in a cave and banned from NHS care.'

PCR tests - we read that the inventor of the test, Kary B Mullis, American biochemist, allegedly said that the test was not made to detect any type of infectious disease and was not reliable. Some people tested before they went anywhere, others never took a test.

Restaurants - closed in the first lockdown with only takeaways/ fast food available. When restaurants opened, people walked in with their mask on, took the mask off when they sat down to eat and then put it back on if they got up to go anywhere within the restaurant.

Pinging phones - a hot topic of conversation when the restaurants re-opened! As you went into a restaurant you were asked for contact details - if you had eaten in a restaurant where subsequently someone called in to say they had also eaten there at the same time and had now tested positive for covid... you were called / 'pinged' and found yourself in quarantine and off work for 10-14 days whether you were unwell or not.

Public Toilets - closed during the first lockdown - when re-opened in the men's toilets every other urinal was out of use so that you didn't stand together, meanwhile you often passed someone in close proximity on the way in or out.

Churches - Weddings - Funerals
In March 2020 churches were closed. By June they were able to host individual prayer and funerals with restrictions. Group singing was not allowed. Weddings and Funerals were limited to 30 people with social distancing.

Partying in Downing Street
On 20 May 2020, just an hour before the alleged Downing Street "bring your own booze" party at 6pm, the daily coronavirus news briefing was held urging people to stay alert and control the virus. In the broadcast the general public were told 'you can meet one person outside your household in an outdoor public place, provided you stay two metres apart'. The big question is 'Why did they feel safe to have parties in the middle of a pandemic when they had closed the country down?'
What did they know that they weren't telling us?
While parties took place in Downing Street ... friends and family were not allowed to go into one another's homes or gardens - social distancing meant couples and relatives who lived apart were not allowed to hug each other. People were threatened and fines issued to those who broke the rules.

Democracy in the UK - 13 December 2022 & 20 October 2023, Andrew Bridgen speaks on the potential harms of mRNA vaccines.'Since the roll-out in the UK of the BioNTech-Pfizer mRNA vaccine, we have had almost half a million yellow card reports of adverse effects from the public. It is more than all the yellow card reports of the past 40 years combined.' He spoke on both occasions to a virtually empty chamber.
Another big question 'Why Won't Anyone Discuss This?' Whatever our individual views are surely an open debate is the normal way forward.

And much much more ...

Did we really think we could come back from all of this and life would carry on as it had before?

Looking back, I wonder what you think of the restrictions... some will think we weren't restricted enough, others that most or all restrictions were necessary and some will think that the restrictions made no sense at all.

*If you would like to share your memories please contact me at www.memoriesoflockdown.com

'We don't all see things the same way'.

## Dave

Thinking back to March 2020 when the pandemic started - seeing news reports of people in China walking down the street, shaking in agony and dropping dead - fake type videos - what the hell!

Lockdowns began and during the first 3 weeks I didn't really believe it or care too much about it, I didn't wear a mask or use hand sanitiser. I carried on as usual but saw people around me wearing the masks and I wondered if maybe there was something going on! However, another 3 weeks on and I thought that something was definitely going on and in my opinion it was a lot of scaremongering.

I was working in the maintenance side of the 'care' industry - a key-worker so worked through it all. The care sector enforced masks before other sectors. At the beginning, a lot of members of staff stayed on the premises so they couldn't take the illness back and forth. A few people fell ill, no difference from seasonal flu and I took 6 or 7 of them to testing centres; sitting amongst people at the testing centres I never caught anything, I wore a mask under my nose so that I could breathe properly. I would not wear a mask over my nose as we know that the masks are made from fibre glass particles which aren't good for humans to inhale.

As the months went on there was talk of Pharma companies developing vaccines, and as soon as I heard of that I knew it wouldn't be long before a vaccine was released and then mandated especially in the care home setting.

As I had had a polio vax and another on the same day when I was 13 or 14 years old and had suffered a bad reaction, I spoke to my GP and he gave me a vax exemption document. As time went on the vax was released and then mandated to the care home sector; there are 300 employees in the group I work in and I was the only one who was exempt. Another worker refused to have it and lost his job. It was good I thought of it in advance - a lot of people later asked for exemptions from their GPs and were refused. The GPs got £25 per vax so total conflict of interests - follow the money.

GPs have to read the data sheet about the product they are administering and therefore are aware that there should be 3 phases of studies on the product in place, and in this case phase 3 ends at the end of 2023/beginning of 2024. I knew all along that GPs were breaking their oath by giving the vax without phase 3 studies of long term side effects being completed, and it makes it clear how corrupt everything is. The GPs would lose their jobs if they didn't comply.

I saw a lot of hesitancy, but when you have to pay rent or a mortgage and put food on the table for your family you feel you have no choice, though 50.000 people walked out of their jobs in the care sector.

I have researched flu and common colds and those airborne viruses do not spread easily by people sitting next to one another. I believe you can't have a good immune system if you're not exposed constantly to common illness - isolating and locking down everyone for 2 years ruined many people's immune systems, which means that now for those people, if they catch a common cold it will likely be ten times worse than it would normally have been as their immune system has been weakened.

I started looking for all the information, not just what we were being told on the nightly News; I found several social media groups and the UK Column News which was interesting and refreshing to hear what I considered well researched other points of view. All the consistent brainwashing and scaremongering made me start to question everything.

Then - social media platforms started discrediting and blocking scientists who did not agree with the main narrative. Democracy gone!

I cancelled my TV licence and haven't listened to the mainstream News since; anything that only repeats one side of the story with no discussions or debates is of no interest to me.

The pandemic, in some respects, was a good thing as it made many more people start to question everything and wake up to what's actually going on in governments across the world. Mainstream media in the pockets of Big Pharma and Big Corps - the WHO - all with a complete disregard to the people and the people's health; some still think Bill Gates is a philanthropist. Follow the money and you find the Truth. Your health is literally the last thing on their agenda - all you have to do is look back on history; the only way governments can control the people is by fear, whether it's war, pandemics, climate change - that is when government has total control - people in fear are easy to control.

I wasn't able to attend any of the protests in London but know a lot of people who did. People would film and post on social media, there were millions of people protesting - so many people aware and awake - none of it shown on the News. Anything that was shown was minimised showing a few hundred people at the protests and often showing a violent incident which took place at the end of the day by people who had nothing to do with the protest. The ordinary people on the marches included a large percentage of grandparents and many women and children.

I'm expecting a new variant to be pushed out soon - it's a good money-making exercise - however, as the vax was sold to us as a product that would save us from getting Covid and passing it on and we now know it does neither, I am hoping that people across the world will stand up and say 'No' - there is strength in numbers. In some European countries only 20% of people got vaxxed; doctors didn't go ahead with it because there was no research or data to show safety and efficacy.

I knew about RRR Relative Risk Reduction for these jabs - they are not vaccines - mRNA gene therapies since they started being tested in 2005/2006. If people knew they were taking part in an experiment on a product that hadn't been tested with all the potential side effects, knowing it had a 0.1% risk... who would have taken it? Nobody. If the jab had been called by the name it is - 'gene therapy' - people would not have had it so they had to change it to a vaccine, then 3 or 4 months later the term vaccination was changed in the Oxford dictionary and mRNA was classed as a vaccine - changed to make people less hesitant.

*Dave*

The government is there to serve us, not the other way around - people seem to have forgotten this and the government certainly has.

Even before this I was always leaning towards a more holistic, plant-based, water filtrated - natural way of life and when it all happened I couldn't believe they could do it on such a thing on such a big scale.

Good times create weak people and we need to be questioning and always finding out the truth, be strong-minded, The pandemic has created a lot of strong people questioning everything, and the next generation will be even stronger and better equipped for what is still to come.

We will make a better world for our children!

## Sandy

It's a year since I wrote my piece for Rosanne's second book of the trilogy, Memories of Lockdown - the People's Stories, and here is my contribution for book 3.

Very recently I was in west Wales with a good friend, staying in a comfortable yurt on a beautiful piece of land, near a wonderful old church and graveyard. Through a short walk seawards, there is a glorious sandy beach. The weather is dry and hot, the nights are dark with skies full of stars. A red/orange gibbous moon shines down on us full of mystery and we gaze at it with wonder. We swim in the sea and eat well, we have a fire in the evening and listen to the owls, we talk and dream. The autumn berries are starting to ripen around us and we look at amazing shiny new cobwebs on the grass in the mornings.

Now as I write only a short time after our delightful days in Wales I am sneezing and coughing, have no sense of taste or smell, feel exhausted and have tested positive for Covid. It's finally got me as well as many others in the small town in Somerset where I live. I didn't get Covid the first time around and was thankful for that. So this is it! This is Covid, it's still with us. I've had my jabs, all of them. I was due another as apparently I'm 'a priority due to your age' as it said in the text from my GP! Now I've had to cancel the jab and wait for another until 28 days after testing positive, whenever that will be. It feels like my turn of having Covid has gone on for ever - days going by so slowly with not much happening. I've had to cancel or not attend so many events including a friend's funeral, my birthday theatre trip, several appointments, visiting a poorly friend, a yoga day, a family outing and my Covid jab of course!

The seasons have changed. It is now well and truly autumn. The garden is closing down for the winter. The colours are still vivid but sadly I can't detect the wonderful autumn smells because of having Covid. I have taken protecting others seriously. I decided to be careful and not mix with others inside. We did go for a glorious walk on a nature reserve on my birthday and the warden backed off quickly when I told her I had Covid even though we were outside. My family delivered some wonderful goodies and treats so I've enjoyed chocolate and dates, a new book and two gorgeous new soaps. One thing that's been so sad and hard while I've been unwell is listening to the news. It's almost unbearable to hear about the conflicts in parts of the world like Ukraine and now Palestine and Israel. The suffering, the refugees with nowhere to go. The violence and anger is hard to hear. I constantly wonder why people find it so hard to find peaceful ways to resolve conflicts, to enable us all to share and live harmoniously. I spend my time feeling uneasy about the future, about the future of humanity as a whole. Then I hear some hopeful positive voices and little chinks of light seep in and I believe once again that conflicts can be resolved. Finding compassion and living in harmony is possible, but it seems a hard, slow and complex process.

The Covid enquiry is well underway, hearing the stories of people whose loved ones died - voices of people who weren't allowed to be with their dying relatives because of the rules at the time. Reminders of the hardship and sorrow so many experienced.

What will we learn from this, what do we ever learn from terrible and difficult circumstances, or from wars and disputes? How can we manage the awareness of other people's suffering? Maybe accepting suffering as well as the positives is part of living, but surely we must try to limit the suffering? What sustains me is my family and friends. I am so lucky to have this support. Being in nature and gardening during my Covid experience has been a lifeline too. Some quiet, slow digging and clearing of the summer beds. Gathering some fresh produce to take home. Finding sustaining poems and articles to read and doing gentle yoga helps keep me present and steady.

## Bob

How could anyone think that closing the world down for 2 years was a good thing?

The only thing it has done is increase excess deaths, mainly caused by vaccine damage, and by the many who have died and will die because they did not get the treatment they needed over the past 3 years. Not to mention the suicides, mental illness, broken marriages and division between families and friends. Brother against brother!

And - guess what? - record profits for the pharmaceutical companies and the millions that have been made by those 'mates' who were handed Covid contracts: half of the government ministers with shares in pharmaceutical companies.

It turns out that the dreaded Covid-19 is just a mutated common cold virus, which is not a problem as long as your immune system is working properly, and that is mostly down to diet, not unproven drugs and 'fast foods' containing all sorts of poisons.

Why we were told to vaccinate our children - who naturally have the stoutest immune system - I will never know; but I could make a good guess! I am 73 and have COPD so am considered 'at risk', but I'm sure I caught it, and I survived. No! I did not have any tests to find out if it was Covid. What was the point? I never tested before to see whether I had flu! Feel ill? – stay at home until you feel better and the fact that you had to pay for a test – as much as £200 - more in the pharma's coffers? No thanks!

People took the vaccines, good people all over the world because they thought it was the right thing to do; it has since come to light that the magic vaccine did none of the things we were assured it would do. It didn't prevent catching it and it didn't prevent the transmission of it. Saying it reduced the effect of Covid is insubstantial as there has to be some sort of comparison, which there obviously wasn't.

Frankly, in light of recent illnesses caused by the vaccines, there seems to have been less chance of actually catching Covid than having vaccine side effects. Needless to say I declined having the vaccine, but I didn't have to travel far, nor work anywhere, so it was my choice. I feel sorry for the people who didn't want it but who were forced into having it or they would lose their jobs.

Interesting that POTUS Trump, for all his failings, knew that ivermectin and hydroxychloroquine were effective in treating Covid, but he was ridiculed and probably forced into silence. It is now proven that he was right. The fact that they were efficacious and cheap? Hmmm!

*Bob*

You can't tell me that there is not a cupboard full of skeletons when it comes to governments and cover-ups. When Joe Bloggs was fearful of even opening his front door because he would drop dead on the spot, and people were not allowed to be with their dying loved ones, there were parties going on in No.10? We have to conclude they knew there was nothing to worry about with this virus. We also know that rule No.1 to those in control is self preservation!

The whole of the world was involved in this obvious crime, including the indigenous people in third world countries who were experimented on:
So!
WHO were pulling the strings?
WHO is better off because of it?
WHO installed fear into the entire population of the world?
WHO is now suggesting that everyone be digitally accounted for?
WHO wants to have total control?
Follow the money!
Oh! Money! That's another thing they don't want you to have.

The real outcome for me is that I don't trust anything I am told by the 'authorities' now, including the mainstream media who are obviously complicit. My trust destroyed! I don't listen to, nor watch the 'news', nor read papers any more. I look into things that interest me and make up my own mind.

I'm sorry for ranting a bit there, but it makes me so angry that it was allowed to happen! And the World Health Organisation is STILL trying to force us into submission.

In my last story I deliberately avoided political and sensitive comments, so I'm making up for it now that this farce is coming to light. Of course people died, but people do die every year from frailty, flu and other morbidities.

During the last year I have made a lot of changes. I sold the family home in Spain and moved back to the UK, something I would never want to go through again - at least not on my own! It was the most traumatic period of my life. I was starting to get depressed and the workload seemed so vast that I came to a standstill, not knowing what to do first, which way to turn.

So now was the time to start packing things up ready for the move. Not being in the best of health I was so lucky that the buyer, a friend, helped me organise everything and with the help of friends the house was packed up! This was my lowest period. I am eternally grateful to them for the help. I think I would still be there now if it wasn't for them. I decided not to take any furniture. It would be cheaper to buy new from IKEA than ship it to UK, but the number of small things seemed to double every time I packed one piece.

The sale was fairly traumatic, in true Spanish style we were clobbered for a whole lot of tax, the town council had changed the rules (of course they had) and we either accepted it or lost the sale. We accepted it but it was a bitter pill to swallow.

The sale went through and I stayed with a dear friend for a few days before flying back to the UK. Ironically I caught the flu at this time and wondered if I was going to have to postpone, but I felt well enough to travel on the morning.

On a lighter note, after leaving Spain in November and arriving back rather ragged in every way, I had a month to recover physically and mentally before Christmas which was perfect. Family in and out and all around. I have a new start and can devote myself to Art which was a seed that germinated and flourished during the lockdown periods. A silver lining.

*Bob*

I am now enjoying my retirement in a beautiful sleepy Somerset town with everything I need within walking distance, and have met some like-minded people involved with sacred geometry, sculpting and energy, which I find fascinating. Being very close to Glastonbury - an artisan town - in my element. I have already participated in a couple of local Art exhibitions and thoroughly enjoyed it, meeting new friends and contacts all the time.

Is it a better world now? I don't think a lot of people would say it is. However, it is for me with my family close by, but still with a bad taste in my mouth of how it came to be.

Draw your own conclusions.

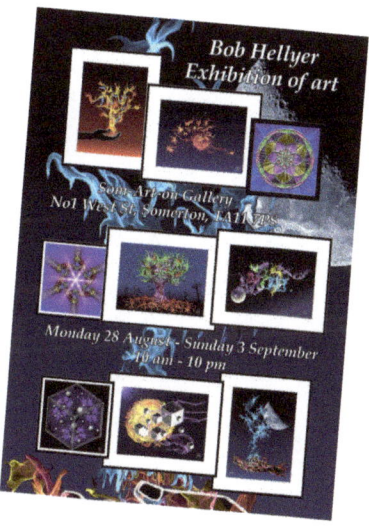

# Chris

**All the things you cannot say**

Anthony Burgess' dystopian novel *A Clockwork Orange* came out the year I was born.

By 2020 I was well on the way to a merry retirement, firmly believing that we would enjoy a lifetime of relative peace in the civilised West.

It was a bright warm day in March that year when the WHO declared a worldwide pandemic. I remember because it was my sister's birthday.
Three days later I came across the late David Crowe's essay 'Does the 2019 Coronavirus Exist?' Crowe was the host of a long-running podcast called The Infectious Myth which I'd been

following for quite a while. Over the years I'd come across a lot of criticism of the standard medical dogmas, shall we say, and his podcast was particularly good.
By the time I'd read Crowe's study, twice for good measure, I was well and truly inoculated against Covid propaganda.

One morning at work I bumped into the normally bolshy Rosemary in the kitchenette preparing her super-sized cafetière. The topic of Covid was in the air.
"Are you following the news?" she asked.
"I don't think there's too much to worry about," I replied nonchalantly.
"Well, I don't agree," she replied gruffly, looking like I might've infected her already.
"I'd rather work from home, just to be safe." She picked up her tray of coffee and scuttled off, putting as much space between us as she could.
I could almost smell the terror in the air after she'd gone.

Sitting not far from my desk in our open plan office was Min, a young Korean New Zealander. "It's an epidemic of testing!" I announced out of the blue. "The published science doesn't prove it's a new virus!" I added. She asked to see what I was reading, so I printed off a copy of Crowe's essay for her, but never heard another squeak about it.

Rosemary got her wish soon enough. By late March, nearly everyone was working from home. We were fortunate to be classified as an essential industry, and so I carried on at home with barely a hiccup. One downside was missing my daily commute by bike which was keeping me fit and trim.

With the alert levels dropping in May, and again in June, weekend cycling with the mates was back on the programme.

At Espresso Workshop with the boys at the end of our Saturday morning ride I ask, "Is anyone really worried about this Covid thing?"

Murray works in the health system, though is not a physician. "There are a lot of very smart medical people all over this, a lot smarter than me, and they are taking it really seriously," he said.

As 2020 progressed, we could hear the thundering hooves of the three horsemen of the apocalypse edging ever closer from beyond the global horizon. Pfizer, J & J, Moderna. Pfizer, one of the most criminal corporations in history.

No one I knew was getting sick, except in the head maybe. We didn't have television at home, didn't listen to public radio, so our brains avoided the daily cycle of wash, rinse and repeat.

I knew that the Spanish flu had swept through New Zealand in six weeks, leaving a trail of death and destruction behind it. Then it was all over.

So far, all I'd seen with my own eyes were terror tactics of a decidedly unkind sort, and news reports of 'Covid deaths' of a handful of extremely old and frail people.

That August we took a quiet Winter holiday in Kuaotunu, and for the first time thought seriously about moving away from Auckland. The government's house-building programme had turned our neighbourhood into hillsides of raw clay and thumping heavy machinery. A row of new houses looked like a ghetto in the making. The future didn't look rosy in an avenue called Roseman. From our vantage point high on a hill overlooking Great Mercury Island, we discovered that we'd both become depressed by life in the big smoke, but we had no inkling where else we might live. Our life over the years had shrunk to the daily, weekly grind of work; our circle of friends and activities had diminished, and the friends we had we saw all too infrequently. Life had closed in, and the future looked bleak.

On the evening of April 1st the following year, 2021, we pulled into the driveway of our new home on the West Coast, having sold up and said our goodbyes. It was a glorious day as we drove across the island from Picton under a fizzing, radiant sky; there could've been no more ravishing welcome to the South Island, the (big) smoke gone from our eyes.

I set up a rough and ready desk, and carried on providing my essential service from a room with a view of the Paparoa Ranges, thankful to my employer for keeping me on.

Meanwhile, Pfizer had arrived...

Our new neighbours, Rod and Mary, were cheery retirees from Auckland. Rod encouraged me to join the Mens Shed and helped me find my way around the big woodworking machines. Mary was a cheerful character, generous with her time and her information whenever we needed to know something about our new hometown. Occasionally she'd even send over a plate of cupcakes!

"All I know is that there's a terrible virus going around and I don't want to catch it!" my mother declared. She believes the nice man on TV.

She's a robust, healthy, independent woman, living a full life in Queensland. She got the jab. I learnt later that she'd suffered a number of mini-strokes afterwards.

August 2021. I got an email from the local writing group coordinator to confirm that meetings were cancelled because of Level 4 restrictions. The next meeting would be at the library a month later, coincidentally on my birthday — but the library was still closed in late September, so the group met privately. I decided to check it out. I worked up a short poem about my consternation with my sister and took it along. Shaking with nerves, I read it aloud:

> How can I save you from your silly self?
> You're telling me you got the shot knowing it gave mother a stroke?
> I sent you those stats from Australia,
> official government numbers about the danger you're in.
> You sent me... nothing but a polite "how-are-you?"
> from which I learn that you'll never take that pill.
> You'll be rolling up soon to be shot again,
> preferring their medicine to mine.
> I really don't think I can save you from your silly silly self.

"Is that to do with Covid?" someone asked afterwards.
"Yes," I answered.
Silence.
I didn't go back.

One of my Auckland cycling buddies put up a message on our group's WhatsApp page that sounded critical of the Covid responses.
"Great that you can see how crazy the government has got," I chimed in.
"That's phase one," I added. "Phase two is malevolent."
"Oh dear, Chris," wrote Murray.

October 2021, and mandates arrived.

In mid-October my employer announced they were committed to looking after our health and safety. Great. They put out a draft vax policy for feedback. Within the seven-day timeframe, I compiled a 57 page document, 54 of which were an assessment of the risk of the Pfizer vaccine. I went for the sledgehammer approach to knock this thing down!

My colleagues knew about it, but only Min asked for a copy. Again, not a squeak about it afterwards. Our team met via Zoom to share what we thought of the draft policy. Dissent came from only two of us. We both said no jab for me, no matter what.

"I think vaccination is the socially responsible thing to do," Myra declared in her sweet way. This made as much sense to me as saying that I should put on a jumper so that your ski jacket will keep you warm. But by then, not much was making sense anymore.

A week later the policy went live, virtually unchanged. It involved assessing the level of risk for each position. Phew, no worry for me then, since I don't work with clients and can work from the blissful solitude of my living room.

A week later the CEO scrapped it anyway. Now, all visitors to the premises would have to show a vax pass, and when we returned from the summer break in January, we would all have to do the same.

Oh well. Now it was clear they weren't interested in anyone's health, only in following the government's diktat. If anyone got injured by the vax, ACC would pick up the pieces, they said. Russian roulette, in other words.

Fuck.


A number of my Auckland cycle buddies were planning a cycle tour around the top of the South, from Nelson, via the Old Ghost Road, to Westport, then north to the Heaphy and back over to Nelson. We planned to host them en route. Murray was in the mix, but was unsure about including the Old Ghost Road after a bit of online research. I said he could skip it and come early, but as time passed he must've got cold feet about the whole thing. One day he rang and said he'd decided not to do the trip, and explained why. We talked at length about how we view this Covid thing. His doctor friends were his trusted authorities. He didn't want to risk catching it, with a new grandchild in the family. I asked him if he'd looked at the actual figures for the risk, but by then the conversation had become awkward and tense. We were on different sides of the fence. We haven't spoken since.

Christmas was approaching. Lockdowns had been replaced by traffic lights and passes. My sister booked flights to come down to see us. We were anxious about her visit. She is dutiful, uncritical, and would've complied with all the contact tracing requirements of the new system. This would put herself and us at risk of getting caught up in an absurd dragnet and forced into an unnecessary quarantine. I asked her if she'd consider not doing all that if she came down: paying in cash, ignoring QR codes, using a false name and phone number. She cancelled.

The summer holiday was over. I soldiered on in a state of uncertainty, even anxiety at times. The universal vax policy seemed mad to me, and by then I had no confidence that the management had not gone completely crazy. I'd heard through the grapevine that they'd not bothered to read my sledgehammer, and instead just wanted to know who'd written it. In the end it may have helped because as the days and weeks went by, no one said anything, and while nearly all of my colleagues complied, I carried on working from home, left in peace.

Well, kind of in peace. What if one of my colleagues had a bad reaction to the shots? My warnings to my manager about the risks had fallen on deaf ears too. She was intent that everyone in her household should be vaccinated, including the grandchildren. Later in the year she let us know that her sister had died suddenly. Of course, you can't say anything.

March 2022. No café for you lot! So we started our own, a weekly coffee club in friend's houses. Soon we found ourselves being more social than we'd ever been.

I made a tactical blunder. The guys at the Mens Shed volunteered to help repair some Council houses for flood victims. Before being told what to do we were given a Health and Safety briefing. First a video presentation, and then a pile of paperwork to read and sign. "We'd be assuming you've all got your vax passes with you," said the supervisor.
"Well that counts me out," I said.
Dead silence.

I was banned from the Mens Shed for months afterwards. Turns out they'd had a meeting about vax requirements that I knew nothing about.

Rod never referred to the fact that I wasn't at the Mens Shed anymore, but he rang one day to say he was driving Mary over to Christchurch hospital. Her cancer, which had long been in remission, was back. The weeks passed, they came and went, until they were no longer coming, at least not together. We never saw Mary again. Rod told me what the doctors had told him: "We've never seen cancer flare up again so fast and so aggressively before." We knew it was hopeless when she went into a hospice. A few weeks later we attended her funeral. Since then 'turbo cancers' have become a thing. Of course, I never said anything.

Eventually I went back to the Mens Shed. Richard said to me, "I'm sorry how it all worked out." He was the only one, but I was grateful. I carried on as if nothing had happened, but of course it had.

Everyone in my immediate family had another birthday during 2022, I'm glad to say. Can't say the same for the in-laws, though.

In the Spring that year I turned 60. We celebrated with a large number of our new friends. On that very day, I later learned, the life of two-time Booker Prize winner Hilary Mantel was suddenly snuffed out after a stroke. Off she went to join Anthony Burgess in the land of eternal peace.

Now that dystopia is regime policy all across the West, the prospect of a merry retirement looks rather less assured, and there is a little part of me that wasn't there back in 2020: a tiny secret envy that Anthony and Hilary had made their escape in time.

Ah, but that's just the devil whispering in my ear.
"yarbles, bolshy great yarblockos to thee and thine"
Thanks, but no thanks.

# Carol

*Edith Wellington 1922 - 2017*

This poem is dedicated to our all our precious elders, and especially those who were isolated during Lockdown and felt lonely and abandoned.

   It was inspired by the huge frustration Mum experienced when trying to speak on the telephone to my sister, Andrena Forrest, whenever she called from Australia, where she was living at the time.

*The hands that used to hold me when I was very small*
*Found it hard to hold a phone and make or take a call*
*The ears that used to listen when I went out to play*
*Found it hard to hear my voice and what I had to say*
*So, sad and isolated, it caused my Mum much grief,*
*Her happiness had been stolen by a callous, thoughtless thief.*
*But then along came a hero, who gave the thief a swipe*
*Restored the love and laughter, and the hero's name was... Skype!*
*Thanks to video technology, a truly modern wonder*
*Every day she could chat away to my sister in 'Down-under,'*

*And when Mum saw Andrena and the two of them could speak*
*She would be so happy, she'd light up like Christmas week!*
*It gave them so much pleasure, they had the biggest smiles,*
*And it was clear for all to see that Love can transcend miles.*

*So that was our inspiration and we knew we had to start*
*Creating for our old ones ideas that touched the heart*
*That's why we thought of CheeruP in memory of our Mum*
*To cherish our precious elders and ensure that life is FUN!!*
*It all began with Edith and her problems on the phone*
*The idea is for CheeruP Champions to help folk feel less alone*
*By sharing memories, fun and laughter, video links and more*
*And helping them stay connected with the loved ones they adore.*
*So if we all greeted each elder with a really lovely smile*
*Imagine the happiness that would spread in just a little while*
*And I am fairly certain that before the day is through*
*Every smile you've given out will get given back to you!!*

Carol Pool

CheeruP is an acronym for:
**C**herish **H**onour & **E**ngage **E**lders with **R**espect **U**pliftment
& **P**ositivity with **C**ompanionship, **H**umour, **E**ntertainment,
**E**ducation, **R**esources, **U**nderstanding and **P**layfulness

CheeruP Champions and Bereavement Befrienders are both part of a new charity dedicated to enhancing people's lives and easing the experience of death and bereavement. You can find Bereavement Befrienders on FB.

# Michael Flannagan

Where Do We GO From Here?

Things are back to normal, at least that's what they say. Funny how I still find myself feeling slightly nervous when the bus or the metro is overly crowded. I guess it takes time to negate the Covid fears that we've lived with. It's only normal. It is nice to be hugged again, and I never thought the time would come when I would yearn for such simple moments of tenderness. That's one of the things that's made such an impression on me. Our shared Covid experience has made me more aware of the importance of showing our affection, to show that we care, that we need, that we have longings, and the necessity of trust.

In my opinion, the breakdown of societal trust was the most significant damage caused by the Covid years. Afraid to touch for fear of infection leaves its mark, but it's refreshing to see how the world is slowly moving back to where it was before the outbreak. Life is getting back to normal, and now, it's odd being in a crowd and seeing the anomaly—the lone person still wearing a mask. Are they ill? Are they at high risk for themselves or loved one. These are the questions I ask myself and would like to ask the masked stranger. I never thought wearing a mask could be a conversational starter, but I don't dare because I know it would put the other person on the defensive, and everyone should have the right to make decisions about their life.

It's only normal that a crisis within a society brings about significant changes. That's to be expected; history has taught us that, but unfortunately, many, especially in politics, big business, and the money-making machine have attempted to take advantage of the sensitive position the world is in to further instill mistrust in our once stable institutions. The pharma industry has raked in enormous profits; the political world is still using Covid as a means of division; theorists are still presenting various ideas.

I don't think we're finished with Covid. That would be far too utopian. Just as the world is still dealing with the after effects of colonialism, slavery, apartheid, and other hurdles society has had to overcome, so will we have to deal with Covid. The health aspects may not be as grave as they were three years ago, but there are other challenges we have to face as a society.

There will always be those who will jump at the first opportunity to take advantage of a situation, but I believe if we do what's possible to protect the unifying element and, as individuals, try to make a difference as best we can, we'll get through this and strengthen the bond that holds us together.

I made a pact with myself that I would, despite what comes, keep a positive outlook, because that is the one thing, I am 100% responsible for.

*Memories of Lockdown - 3rd book of the trilogy*

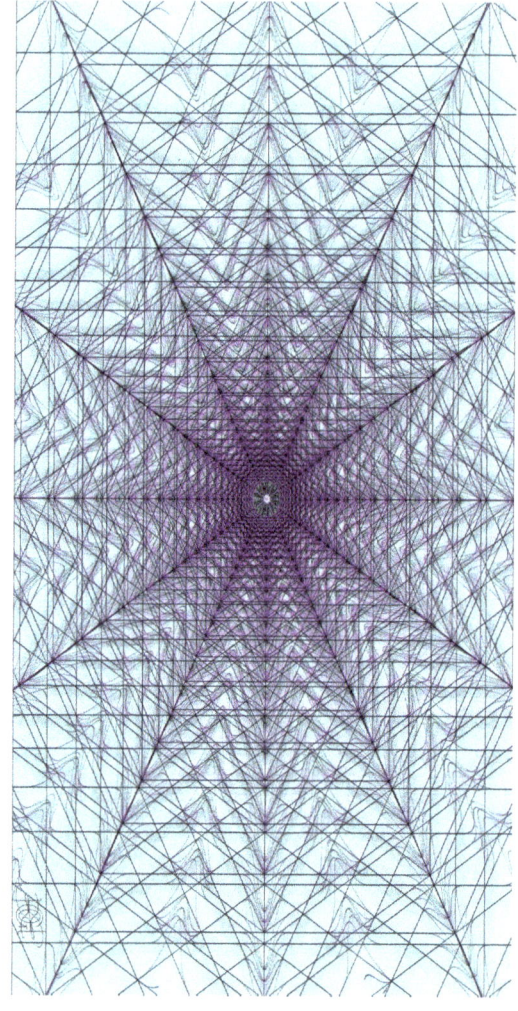

# *Kat*

**Forever Wild, Moon Child.**

I am writing this overlooking the Indian Ocean in Port Louis, Mauritius. I can see people happily drinking their coffee and cocktails, eating samosas or ice creams or croissants and chatting, laughing, flirting. The 'most lethal pandemic in human history' was not only a complete damp squib but is also ancient history. A blip in our short lives where no lessons will be learnt and all the many, many inconsistencies and nonsensical rules will be filed under 'Oops' whilst our governments distract us with the latest pet hysteria. Russia, monkey pox, global warming tweaked to climate change and of course a new and improved and scary Covid variant for winter. I try to avoid online main stream media but I do enjoy a leisurely perusal of the public comments and it does give me hope that the most liked is usually the one insisting

The Covid Ship has sunk and support for lockdowns and masks and hastily devised jabs has sunk with it.

In many ways the last 3 years has been a mourning process. I started with denial, they won't actually destroy the economy for a virus with a 99% survival rate (aka flu)? Will they? Then when they did, with their hollow promises of it's just 3 weeks, it's just to flatten the curve, it's just a mask, it's just one, no two, no three, no four jabs and we never actually said they stopped transmission (you did)... I quickly reverted to anger. And this was a prolonged phase which I can still occasionally feel dormant. Just recently a stranger recognised that I carry 'low level anger' with me.

According to the web the next mourning stage is bargaining. This is when we realise there is nothing we can do individually to influence the juggernaut, but we want to try and gain some control. This was my phase of creating bracelets for every month of Covid restrictions - and as you can see from the photo I am still stubbornly wearing all 24 to this day. My skin is porcelain white underneath them and I genuinely have to blow-dry my arm in the winter after a shower or they won't dry. I look at them daily and they remind me of my resistance to The Rules (or mere 'guidelines' if you're a government official and you've been busted breaking them). I learnt the power of a firm "I'm exempt" followed by a disinterested French shrug of the shoulders because, for me, this was the end of the ridiculous conversation. During this time I did feel very alone, even hated, as the "Covid denying anti-vaxxer conspiracy theorist."

Which is why the next stage was probably depression! When I realised that what was happening - the loss of basic freedoms - was unavoidable. My bargaining hadn't influenced anything and our reality was yet another winter looming ahead with repeat hysterical and fictional narrative to suit. Schools were shut, my job was in jeopardy, my relationship had ended and my friendship circle was barren. I don't believe I stayed in depression very long, it wouldn't have been fair on my children who have the image of formidable, hard working and motorbike riding mother ("Not normal" in their words).

So that leads me quickly into the final stage of acceptance. I do feel more at peace and I am proud of myself for embracing a little bit of independent critical thinking and ignoring the unrelenting propaganda and peer pressure. I am now firmly part of the problematic minority who are going to question absolutely everything going forward.

Why does paying £12.50 to enter London help the climate?

Why do the elite get to enjoy flying in their private jets and eating foie gras in Davos but expect us to own nothing and be happy with the occasional treat of an insect snack and heating only on special occasions?

Are electric cars really better for the environment or do they strip the Congo of cobalt using child labour?

Is oil actually running out?

Why is the Great Barrier Reef at the highest level of coral since records began?

Why is arctic ice cover now increasing when we were told it should have completely melted and obliterated the Maldives (who have just built a brand new runway) and flooded London by now?

Is it possible that humans aren't as clever as we think we are and/or are mostly motivated by money and power and not the greater good of us 'useless eaters'?

But I do try not to dwell on these 'problems not really problems' that the media feed us day and night.

I have a new love in my life and she is beautiful and formidable and 'Not Normal'. She is also the first She I have ever dated and on reflection (and begrudgingly) I suppose I should thank lockdown for her…

I previously wrote about getting my motorbike licence as pushback against inane rules. Well it turns out that a skinny woman on a chunky 1000cc red and white motorbike draws attention. I bored my friend for 2 months whilst I procrastinated over whether being called 'sexy' in my leather biker jacket by another woman was flirtatious or not. Is 'sexy' a strong term? Would you use the word sexy? Maybe she's just being friendly. Hang on… am I sexy? Aren't I 'Just a middle-aged Mum?' Should I text her? What will our ex-husbands say… (I can report that they've both been very supportive).

I haven't recovered all the lost friends from lockdown, two in particular are closed chapters. You know when birthdays come and go without a WhatsApp message and a flippant emoji cake/balloon it's a sign 'it's over'. My children appear content as much as children ever do. Obviously everything is unfair and I don't understand what it's like and they 'Need Snapchat' and most of my accurate and balanced observations are greeted with hysterical OMG you can't say that anymore!

It's been almost four years since Covid-19 infiltrated our lives and it's somewhat ironic that the only thing that has completely unaffected me is the actual virus. The only thing I wasn't scared of was the actual virus. It baffles me that people are still testing and proudly pronouncing they are 'positive' (again!) but they are absolutely certain it would have been so much worse this time if they hadn't had their jabs because 'science' #survivor. So whilst these people are stuck in their doom loop, I've started not just a new chapter of my life but a brand new book - written in a *quirky, stylised and brazen font!* If I had subtitles narrating my day I'd hope they wouldn't be in predictably mundane Times New Roman. When pondering how to describe the personal quirky font I'm envisioning, I asked for 'classy with a touch of Alice in Wonderland'.

With inquisitive Alice in mind, I'm excited and slightly apprehensive about the rabbit holes I may fall down, the Cheshire cats I have yet to meet, and of course I already consider this world to be governed by self-congratulating Mad Hatters. Equally, like Alice, I shall endeavour to remain politely obstreperous, sceptical of authority and ready to believe six impossible things before breakfast.

I said to my girlfriend that frankly there's too much talky talky and not enough kissy kissy on this planet, and whilst I appreciate this isn't a particularly profound way to sign off my trilogy... I'm going to do it regardless.

Stay Wild Moon Child

# Deborah Jane Sutton

**Heaven on Earth is already here.**

Don't be discouraged by world events, don't lose faith in our ability as humanity to create Heaven on Earth.

As an Intuitive Energy Healer who has had the honour and pleasure of reading Soul Profiles and Cards for numerous souls, I can tell you, first hand, that Heaven on Earth is being manifested right now!

For some it is already a reality, For Heaven on Earth is not a place but a level of consciousness.

I have read for part-time healers who are inspired to give up the day job and focus their energy more fully on their healing gifts.

I have read for gardeners who are passionate about growing organic vegetables and delivering them to others.

I have read for gardeners who hold the vision of creating beautiful gardens and opening them up to mental health patients so they can be nurtured by the smells of the plants and the touch of the soil.

I have read for musicians who are inspired to heal others through their music.

I have read for medical technicians who are passionate about guiding the medical industry into more holistic methods.

I have read for those who understand their gifts lie in catering to the basic needs of others, particularly the very young and the elderly.

I have read for animal lovers who are passionate about catering to the needs of animals.

I have read for animal owners who hold a vision of inviting inner city kids to learn about 'life on the farm'!!

I have read for compassionate souls whose purpose it is to spread their loving energy to all those they come into contact with, as well as those they connect with purely through thought.

I have read for those whose passions lie in helping others connect with their physical bodies through physical activity, yoga, dance and outdoor adventures.

I have read for interior designers who are inspired by Feng Shui to add greater healing to their designs.

I have read for builders who are ready and willing to start building houses, communities, activity centres...

I have read for truth seekers whose purpose it is to open the eyes of humanity.

I have read for Hypnobirthers who are passionate about bringing more love and holistic care back into childbirth.

I have read for parents who are homeschooling and hold a vision for an education system that puts their children's welfare first.

I have read for school teachers who are inspired to create an education system that does just that.

I have read for school staff and parents alike, who want to see children nurtured in their innate channel of creativity.

I have read for leaders who are passionate about leading by example for the highest good of all.

I have read for people who are passionate about learning more, understanding more about the energetic universe we live in and raising their vibrations.

I have read for the souls waking up at this time and it touches my heart.

I feel so blessed to be able to affirm and confirm their gifts, dreams and visions.

I feel so blessed to be able to help others, in any small way, step into their divine power and purpose. For in doing so, I step into mine.

Thank you, thank you, thank you.

Heaven on Earth is in the making.

Trust me, I know. It's in the cards!

Heaven on Earth is right here.

You just have to choose it.

## Dr. Diane Bolden-Taylor

There I was going in and out of doctor's offices and medical clinics - the same spaces where Covid patients could be found.

Stepping back for a moment and setting the scene... It was in a costume shop in Bonn, Germany back in 1980 that I found out I had a curvature of my spine; I found a doctor and was diagnosed with scoliosis and sent off to physical therapy. I was also told that at this point I did not need surgery but that I needed to pay more attention to how I stood.

In Munich, 1989, I met my husband, Hollis, an American who was stationed in Germany and at 39 became pregnant for the first time. My obstetrician informed me that combining scoliosis with pregnancy can lead to worse back pain than a typical pregnancy. He hoped I would be strong enough to carry my baby full term. Rachel, my daughter must have sensed that she needed to take care of her mom because she arrived two weeks early and was a whopping 4 lbs 8 oz heavy. How is that for divine intervention! She is a healthy 32-year-old today.

I spent over 17 years travelling throughout Europe where I performed operas and concerts in countries including Switzerland, Germany, Spain, Italy, France, and Austria. Never during that entire time did my back issues cause me any notable pain.

It was early in 2017, long after I had relocated back to the US and began teaching at a university in Colorado, that I began experiencing debilitating pain in the lumbar region of my back and by November 2021 there was no getting around it, I needed back surgery.

The first cases of Covid were discovered in China in 2019 and we were just learning how dangerous (possibly deadly) this disease was.

Here in the US conversations about the Covid pandemic began in January of 2020 and the highest peak in hospitalizations occurred in December 2020, and 2021 aligning with the largest peak in reported case rates. On March 11, 2020 the World Health Organization (WHO), declared the novel coronavirus (Covid-19) outbreak a global pandemic.

Everyone was coming and going wearing their masks, washing their hands, using sanitizer, and keeping their distance from others whenever possible. The fist bump was used instead of hugs and kisses when greeting someone. Early in 2021 my whole family and I (except for 4-year-old granddaughter, Deja) took the necessary vaccinations to help shield ourselves from this horrible virus. Nevertheless, we all came down with the Covid-19 virus. Perhaps it was Deja who brought the virus home to us from preschool? Who knows! We quarantined and managed to recover within a week and a half - thank God!

I stopped teaching the occasional voice students who would typically come to my house for lessons. There was data advising that singing in a room for an extended period of time in close contact with one or more persons, and little ventilation was a recipe for disaster. Singers and certain wind and brass instrumentalists evidently generate respiratory aerosols at high rates. In other words when blowing air, they spew a lot of droplets into the space around them. How upsetting it was to hear that choruses had to resort to meeting per Zoom, everyone in their own home! How sad I was to hear from so many of my professional singer friends who depended on their operatic and concert engagements, that from one day to the next their contracts were cancelled.

Broadway was shut down, opera programs for young singers and places like the Metropolitan Opera halted productions. Live performances at weddings, and funerals were halted! Actually, there were some funeral homes that had drive-by viewings of bodies - imagine that! Church services were no longer in person but per Zoom. There I was at home giving myself the wine and bread for communion - so sad! However, one positive thing about the church Zooms was that there were many online meetings, my favourite being our church's Conversations on Race. What an eye-opener it was to hear how so many people felt about white privilege and wanting to learn about and be more sensitive to the needs of minorities.

Our family outings were no longer to go to the movie theater but to the grocery store. We would all pile into the car to go to the store to collect toilet paper and sanitizer among other necessities. Seeing all the empty shelves was very disturbing. Many items like chicken, meat, vegetables, bottled water, and even soap were in limited supply! Since this was during the height of Covid, the hospital was overcrowded with patients who needed immediate assistance. Most hospitals were only performing outpatient surgeries at that time. My Doctor assured me that I could have my surgery early in the morning and after recovery be on my way back to Greeley that same evening; that would make me an outpatient.

Anschutz Medical Campus is the largest academic health Center in the Rocky Mountain Region. It is a huge complex and while I was there during the height of Covid, every available space was occupied with patients including the ends of each of the corridors on each floor, sections of the waiting rooms, cafeteria, and even the observation tower.

So, on November 10th, 2021, I went in for surgery on my lower back. On the way to the operating room, I prayed that God would protect me and guide the hands of the surgeon and others who were caring for me. The surgery was at 8am and I was on my way home to Greeley by 6pm that same day.

Thank God for my husband Hollis, my daughter and my 4-year-old granddaughter who were more than happy to care for me.

My sister would be coming from Illinois to visit us for Christmas so I was happy that I would have approximately 5 weeks prior to her arrival to gain some mobility. I was thrilled that I would be home for Thanksgiving too. Typically, I would have made the homemade

dressing, green bean, Irish potatoes, and turkey leg vegetable dish and side salad; however, Hollis is a great cook so I knew he would be happy to prepare everything including the turkey. Early on Thanksgiving day I awoke with the most excruciating headache; it was discovered that at the site of the incision in my lower back a liquid was oozing out! Off to the emergency room we went. So, from Saturday, November 25, 2021, until Monday, December 6, I remained in the hospital with all manner of machines and tubes inserted into my body. However, I was in a beautiful big hospital room complete with a television and a wonderful view of the sky which allowed me to see sunrises and sunsets.

My caregivers, including a lovely infectious disease Doctor popped in to see me and to check on my progress, but also to hear stories about my travels in foreign countries, the operas I had sung, the audiences for whom I had sung, the size of the concert halls I had sung in, and the orchestras and conductors I had been fortunate to work with. They wanted to hear all of it, and since I was a captive audience and loved expressing how grateful I was for my many experiences, I loved chatting with them!

My infectious disease Doctor said she had never really been anywhere outside of the country but meeting me had inspired her to add that to her wish list. She, like so many others I had spoken with, was inspired to be courageous enough to try something new in her life.

The many conversations I had with the hospital personnel distracted me from focusing too much on the fact that I couldn't even go to the bathroom without having someone assist me. I had no privacy as I tried to relieve myself. Oh well, such is life in a hospital!

Just as I was starting to feel better my Doctor, who was German and got a kick out of the fact that I speak the language, entered my room to tell me some upsetting news. When he started with "Es tut mir lied (I am sorry...) I knew I had to brace myself for what was coming. He said I had bacteria growing in my body where the incision for my operations was located. He explained that he needed to open me up again to clean out all bacteria growing there!

My response was "Do what you must do to make me well and whole again! I was put under (given anesthesia!) for the third time in 3 weeks and was operated on yet again! Hollis and Rachel had been coming to visit me daily, though not together - only one visitor was allowed on any given day. Thank God for all the Doctors, and other hospital staff that stopped by to see me frequently. There were calls from my pastors, friends, and former students as well! I didn't have time to get bored or depressed.

The third operation on my back went as planned. One hitch though - they had difficulty waking me up from the anesthesia, They called Hollis and advised that he should get to the hospital right away.

I am so grateful that I know how good God is and how praying can bring peace of mind. I asked God to heal me, remove all bacteria from my body and allow me to continue my life, with my family and friends, away from the hospital. Yet I also prayed that God's will be done, not mine. If he chose to call me home to be with Him, then I was open to that as well. Still, I am so thrilled to be here among the living.

Hollis later explained to me that this particular trip to the hospital was one of the worst trips he has ever had to make, he didn't know that I wasn't coming out of the anesthesia, just that there was an issue related to the operation. However, by the time he reached the hospital I was slowly waking up. As one could imagine, with all the tubes and other machinery they had me hooked up to, I was a frightening sight to behold.

Of course, I had no memory of any of this - I just thanked God that I was awake again and that they had removed all the bacteria from my body.

When I think of what I would have missed had I not awakened; Deja's first day at Kindergarten, Rachel's promotions at the TV station where she is a producer, our family trips to the mountains that were filled with so much laughter, another chance to perform wonderful music (this time by Ives) with a large group of instrumentalists (the Boulder Concert Band) in front of a big welcoming audience, talks with my sister and two brothers, and laughter with my husband of nearly 34 years.

As if three operations during Covid weren't enough, I managed to fall over my cat (well, Rachel's cat actually) thereby breaking the tibia in my left leg. Yes, I broke yet another bone. Only this time no medical intervention was necessary - I just needed to be non-weight bearing for several weeks until the bone healed. I was surprised that senior citizens can grow new bone! Imagine that!

I am well on the way to recovery now though it has taken almost two years for the nerves in my back and legs to heal. Being able to resume my morning walks in the park near my house and being able to shop in the grocery store without having to lean on the cart for support are signs that I am getting stronger by the day.

As awful as the whole Covid pandemic was, my ordeal with my back surgeries put me in situations where I was constantly reminded of how amazing my life has been, how many people have touched my life and how I, in turn have influenced the lives of so many.

I, like so many others, have been getting back to the business of living each day with joy and great anticipation of what is yet to come.

I sincerely hope that this excerpt from my life story will inspire you to do the same!

# Astrology
*'the language of probability'*

We are moving from the Age of Pisces into the Age of Aquarius. The Age of Pisces has shaped human history for around 2000 years, and is slowly coming to an end, as the Age of Aquarius takes its turn.

The primary values in the Age of Pisces were money, power, control, materialism, ego, competition, separation and external power structures. It was the age of 'Me,' the cult of individuality, and the birthplace of modernization.

The Aquarian Age is here to bring a shift in consciousness, emphasizing unity, intuition, and the recognition of our interconnectedness as a global community. It is a time of spiritual awakening. The Age of Aquarius is a time of new beginnings, major changes, establishing new systems, and speaking our truth.
   It is the age of 'We' not 'Me'. There will be new paradigms of how people can live together in peace and equality.

Within this transition time...
LOVE - time of change - relationships - jobs - friendships - values - integrity - photonic light - solar flares - time of choice - fear - victim - co-creator - transformation - sovereignty - surrender - birthing the New Earth - self LOVE - self nurture - self healing - Unity - Rise of the true gentle power - strong - gentle - humble - barefoot on the grass - sharing - Individual rights & freedoms - expanded awareness - ascension - shifting frequencies - new systems - rebellion - revolution - control - media - letting go of the old - earthquakes - greater equality - eruptions - awakening - discipline - wealth - money - LOVE - banking - currencies - volatility in finance - new financial systems - micro currencies - health - new relationships - different relationships - sharing - community -

decentralised currencies - food production - decentralised travel - manifesting - disclosure - pharmaceutical drugs - Truth - intuition - empowerment - new chapter - new cycles - back into wholeness - joy in simplicity - introspection - new belief system - warrior energy - fighting for what is right - best of times - purifying water - flow of water - power of water - individual power - revelation - greater equality - individual rights & freedom - restless - rebellion - revolution - shocks - freedom - impetuous - LOVE - impatient - corporations - power - compassion - gratitude - Peace - Justice - authenticity - endings - new beginnings - quantum technology - energy - ancient wisdom - individual timelines - balance - letting go - collaboration - soul tribe - like minds - build new world - healing technologies - light technology medicine - unconditional LOVE - regeneration - grounding big ideas - me v we - war & peace - loss - grief - surrender - death - re-birth - communication - speed of development - social media & AI - sociability - plasma - chaos - song - dance - turbulence - tiring - tough times - betrayal - abuse of power - low frequency energy - betrayal by patriarchy - deception - depopulation - ecological damage - pandemic - soul tribe - LOVE

Fast Change Ahead.

# Jan

As my story started with my mum's health issues, I will complete my 3 years story with an update.

All is well, mum is now 87 and kicking and fighting her way through to her 90's and beyond, I hope. She has learnt to live with her heart issues, drinking less gin, eating less cheese, and trying not to worry about the whole world!

The medical help has been fantastic, the care and education has been extremely informative, and we have all learnt some very helpful lessons for not only her health but for us all as we get older.

I look back now at the whole Covid situation and it's hard to believe we were locked up, kept back, and restricted in so many ways. How we all used to watch the evening news for statistics and the latest death rates and scare us all with what was happening globally. I will never know if all the restrictions were necessary, but I do know that I trust the medics and will always trust in them as they saved my treasured mum.

So many people lost their beloved family members and friends due to Covid or other diseases that were recorded as Covid – it was all very tragic and confusing and still is to be honest.

On to December 2022 - My mum travelled by herself down to Perth, Western Australia last December to celebrate with me, my 60th birthday. This was quite something and I will never ever forget this enormous effort and her utter determination to be here for my party. She really is an incredible woman and her ability to never give in is an example of her tenacity and resilience.

To bring you right up to date, August 2023. I have just returned from a month long break back in UK, Greece, and New York – so I travelled extensively to visit many friends and family, no masks, no Covid restrictions and it was a pleasure and fun to travel once again and long may it stay that way.

Can I take this opportunity to thank Rosanne for this trilogy of shared experiences throughout the world with her friends and colleagues. It has personally been a privilege to be asked to be part of this experience and to know that we are now little authors of our own stories and have been published in books is just beyond belief!

Health, happiness, and peace to everyone.

Love, love, love
Jan

## JB

**'So What' - A life lesson in Jazz.**

What to write? I don't know... but then I found myself listening to a Miles Davis classic 'So What'. Now don't be put off by the rather dismissive shrug of the shoulders title. There's more to it than that! There are some life lessons to be had here.

This is a 1950's post-bebop piece played by an acoustic band consisting of drums, double bass, piano, trumpet and tenor sax and is taken from the album 'A Kind of Blue'. It's a fine example of a tight but free flowing unit where everyone gets a chance to do their thing but with respect to the other musicians.

It starts with an infectious riff on the double bass with punctuation by the rest of the band. The drummer uses brushes to keep it subtle and the piano plays short soft stabs, and this provides a perfect platform for the two main soloists.

Miles Davis, trumpet, underplays, undercuts and sneaks into what's going on. Never overpowering anything but keen to explore the possibilities as his solo voice takes off and becomes more strident, more purposeful and when he's done he exits without any fuss.

John Coltrane, tenor sax, enters the fray. Now Coltrane is on a different trip. He's famous for his classic jazz masterpiece 'A Love Supreme' where, over four movements he seeks a kind of spiritual high as he ends in a free form ecstasy. Coltrane ventures a similar path with effortless cascading notes, but like all the band members, a lack of ego keeps the whole band tight.

It's a life lesson of doing your thing and allowing others to do their thing without contention, harmony with each person respecting the others' choices. If only we could all live like that!

I'm doing my thing, you're doing your thing... "So What". Sounds good to me.

## Alison

My Lockdown Journey Part Three.

Wow! What a year!

So much has happened - it's hard to know where to begin. The lies keep spewing from the government and mainstream media like water from a tap that's been left on. Ambulances speed down the streets with their sirens blasting at an almost continuous rate. Yet people never stop to question why. This is not normal. A few years ago questions would have been asked. Now they accept it as if it is perfectly normal. It is not.

Councils keep closing roads and implementing restrictions in towns and cities under the pretence of improving the environment and atmosphere in them. People blindly allow this to happen in the belief that it is reducing carbon footprints, and not realising that it is the first stages of implementing the prisons called 15-minute cities. Those who do voice their concerns are ignored and bulldozered by the Councils, who manipulate figures to suit their cause. Once implemented these cities will be a great source of revenue for the government and their puppeteers. Large fines are planned for those who stray out of their zone. Those who have used up their allocated passes will have to purchase more. If you work outside your 15-minute zone you are going to have a problem… These 15-minute cities (FMC)/Low Traffic Neighbourhoods (LTN)/Ultra Low Emission Zones (ULEZ) are designed to do more harm than good. Increased traffic on the outskirts of towns and cities not only makes it unsafe for children, but causes traffic jams. Slow moving/stationary traffic increases pollution in those areas. The pollution does not stay in situ but drifts into city centres and other neighbouring locations. The environment will suffer. People's health will suffer – respiratory issues, allergies, headaches etc. Most people will not put it down to the poison they are breathing in. They will just put it down to age and other unrelated ailments. Attempts to stop this happening are railroaded by the Councils, the government, and mainstream media. Those who care are being silenced.

What most people seem to have forgotten is that plants need carbon in order to survive. The more carbon dioxide there is the healthier and more abundant the plant life is. The puppeteers do not want this. They want everyone on fake meat, processed foods and GM (genetically modified) vegetables… and bugs. Climate change was created to instil fear over the effects of carbon, and allow more restrictions, taxes and controls to be brought in. They use tools such as chemtrails (planes dumping chemicals in the skies that then form into clouds), HAARP (High-frequency Active Auroral Research Program) that sends out high power radio waves, lasers, and other weapons of mass destruction to manipulate the weather and cause destruction and death. Yes, our planet is suffering, and yes, people are suffering, but it is not due to us. It is due to the antics of the puppeteers. Climate change is manmade. It is fake.

Online shopping is being encouraged. Digital currency is being pushed. Banks are making it difficult for small businesses to bank and withdraw cash. Banks and credit card companies are charging unrealistic fees for card transactions. Businesses are not permitted to pass these charges onto their customers, but HMRC is… CBDC (central bank digital currency) is still being pushed by the government. They still want One World Bank and One World Currency. Banks are closing and freezing businesses and people's accounts for no legitimate or lawful reason. The staff do not know why, and they are powerless to do anything about it. The orders are coming from the top. Banks are losing customers, and yet they do nothing to stop it. Begs the question 'Who is pulling their strings and why, and what back handers are they receiving?'

Small businesses are struggling under the weight of all the restrictions, rent increases and unrealistically large utility bills. There is only so much they can pass onto their customers. Many small businesses have closed. Many more will follow unless people start to support them and fight the authorities and the system.

Cash seems to be making a comeback. People appear to be waking up to the importance of cash. Cash is the key to our freedom, not just of movement, but of voice and choice as well. Many small businesses that had stopped using cash are now accepting it again. They have finally realised the benefits. Cash does not have to be banked. Cash is not traceable unless you want it to be. Cash is not taxable unless you choose for it to be. The banks have made it difficult for businesses and people to bank cash in the attempt to stem the flow and steer people and businesses back to digital. If we stay strong and keep using and banking cash the banks will relent. After all people have the power, especially in numbers.

HMRC (revenues & customs) are in a mess. They are forever changing their processes and forms, leaving people confused and facing penalties and interest charges that are not actually due. People are so fearful of HMRC that they pay without proper investigation or questioning. Helplines are being closed in favour of webchats that are operated by AI (artificial intelligence). The AI in operation has not been programmed to answer most of the queries so issues are not being resolved. More and more of the taxes have to be done through third party software. Self-assessments are due to follow this route soon. Third party software providers keep hiking up their prices as they know they have a captive audience. Not all small businesses are viable enough to absorb this extra cost. Another burden on an already struggling market.

Many small businesses are sole traders, meaning they complete a self-assessment tax return. What most of them do not realise is that self-assessment tax returns are not compulsory. They are in fact a fraud on HMRC's part. The notification is an invitation to complete one. Most people are so fearful of HMRC that they just complete it, file it, and pay over their hard-earned money. HMRC know they are committing a fraud so scare people with notices of fines, penalties, and court hearings. People have the power to say 'No' but they don't so HMRC get away with it.

FEAR is a form of control. HMRC, the government, the media, the large corporations, and the puppeteers know this. Everything they do is designed to keep people in fear so that they can be easily controlled. When enough people lose their fear and stand up to them these entities will crumble and fall. Someone once told me that fear stands for false evidence appearing real. That person was so right.

I lost my fear during my realisation phase (see book one of Memories of Lockdown) when I started reading up on Common Law. Losing this fear enabled me to stand in my sovereignty, and grow. It is very liberating to stand free of the burden of the government, HMRC and other fraudulent authorities.

My journey over the last three years has been huge. It has not been easy. Like so many that have walked beside me, I have been shunned, silenced and abused. I have had my heart broken and watched those that I love suffer needlessly due to the Covid-19 vaccines and fear of authority. They live trapped in their artificial world, working to pay bills they do not need to pay, and obeying orders they do not need to obey, but they are, for now, happy so that is how I will leave them. My attempts to awaken them got me nowhere.

I chose to follow my instincts and my heart. The journey has been turbulent. The realisation phase was tough. I still do not know how I got through it, but I did. That was followed by the action phase – going to rallies, holding up yellow boards and talking to people – in the hope of waking them up to the madness that was going on around us.

At the end of 2022 I went to my last rally. I did not know it was my last one. I fully intended to take them up again in 2023 but it did not happen. January 2023 came and went, and so did February. I found I had no desire to go to rallies. It seems that that phase of my journey was over.

I was still doing the Yellow Boards, every Friday and Saturday. That was still important to me. In December 2022 we lost a comrade in arms. His passing was sudden and unexpected. It left us shocked and numb, with so many unanswered questions, that still remain. In June 2023 the organiser of the Frome Yellow Boards made the decision to stop them. I have to say I was relieved. I was struggling to find the time for them due to other commitments. Also, Extinction Rebellion and Stop Oil had started to copy the yellow boards for their fake causes. Never a good sign.

By this time, I was very much involved with Anna von Reitz, the Jural Assemblies and the different jurisdictions. I also had a heavy workload. Most of my spare time was taken up with learning about how our ancestors were abducted from the land and soil jurisdiction and placed in the air and maritime jurisdictions, how the fraud is still occurring today and how we can extract ourselves from it. I learnt about how our history was altered to suit the puppeteers' agenda, how our schools were used to brainwash children, and how music and the arts were used to brainwash adults.

I also learnt that Charles was not crowned King of England. He was crowned Emperor of Rome making him a servant of the Pope. He could not be crowned King of England as he had sworn his allegiance to the WEF (World Economic Forum). Charles is also the instigator of the climate change agenda.

Not wanting to keep all this important information to myself I did talks and encouraged people to do their own research. I tried to give them hope by showing them a way to a better, free-er, and lawful future in a community that cared about the people. A future that was controlled by the people for the people. A future full of light, love, and harmony.

I was also back studying again. My love for animals has not diminished. In fact, it has grown stronger. They are such amazing creatures that put up with so much without complaining. This year I have been learning a new method of animal healing, and animal communication. My desire to help them is so strong that I have set up an animal well-being business and have been promoting that. I hope next year to be able to drop the accountancy/bookkeeping business and to be doing solely animal well-being.

For the first time since moving into my home in 2001 I have had both the time and money to do the place up. I have spent much of this non-existent summer doing DIY and gardening. Years of neglect due to heavy workloads and lack of time had left my house and garden in dire need of TLC (tender loving care). I have a feeling I will be moving next year and believe I have been given this time to fix my place up in preparation for the move. Where to and when exactly I do not know.

Three years ago I would never have thought I would be where I am now, a free woman standing on the land and soil jurisdiction. Free from all the taxes, rules, and other fraudulent activities instigated by the corrupt authorities. It has been quite a journey.

I end this story as the only living woman currently standing, beside a handful of living men, on the land and soil in the land and soil jurisdiction of England, a sovereign nation. I know I will soon be joined by others ready to reclaim what is rightfully theirs and build a community, government, and a lawful system for the people by the people.

# Shelley

So much has changed in the last year... lots of happy events - Neal turned 60, planning our daughter's wedding, financially things have improved and our Frank turned 2!

And some really tough stuff which we are dealing with on a day to day basis - our celebrations for Neal's birthday were limited because he was caring for his mum who has since passed away from cancer, whilst dealing with his own health issues, and now we are caring for his dad who has dementia - currently looking for a care home home for him as he is not safe to live alone anymore.

On the bright side, travelling seems to be back on the agenda for most people and so we are getting on with life, appreciating all the small stuff which has now become the big stuff!

It's hard to be positive some days but we do - wedding plans are exciting and Frank is a JOY!

## *Aisling Mary Melchizedek*

Beautiful reader, here is the continuation of our wonderful stories, it is such a pleasure to share and express from my heart all that has been going on since story two. Let us dive in, allow your mind to be the neutral observer as you read along, to perceive the energies between the lines which carry frequencies and messages for your further expansion on all levels.

I would like to thank all these beautiful souls that have reached out to me after reading book two, wanting to receive the Vax clearing I offer, it fills my heart to know that they now are feeling so much better with it having been cleared out of their systems.

Here in Spain, it feels that the P(l)andemic and Covid has been totally forgotten and been wiped out of the memory of all. No one speaks about it any longer, all have gone back to lead their lives, many with poison in their bodies from the Vax and a few others without it, like me. Some are still living with side effects from the Covid they went through. I think I caught it too, I did not confirm it as I refused to have a PCR test done. The symptoms were pretty like the ones they spoke about, like losing taste and smell and I was unwell for 2 weeks, so I assume it was Covid. It gave me time for introspection and research, and in the end, I was happy I caught it, so I had built antibodies for those viruses. Sometimes I am still unsure if I believe it to have been a virus or if simply being bombarded nonstop from all sides about it (although I hardly listen to the media), weakened my immune system and I allowed and consented for whatever reason to become ill. It may be a subconscious program running in our mind, needing a break, or looking for attention from others as we are ill. Feel into what it was for you!

All I can say is that here in Spain, foreigners equally as Spanish residents, were really very easy to influence by the media as all ran to queue to get the jab and/or the PCR test easily. I hardly saw or heard people standing up and saying 'no' to it all, that of course made it more difficult for me to convey my message and stand by what I believed to be true. There were many getting annoyed, triggered, and angry when I spoke my personal truth, not willing to even listen but burst out in their opinion about it all. I ended up keeping my thoughts to myself and connecting with likeminded people which did feel more aligned with my own beliefs and thoughts and values in this regard.

I observed how my 'wanting to help syndrome' was guided by my Ego mind in the beginning of it all, I thought I could change people's perspectives and it took a while for me to realize that I needed to respect their opinions and free will choice too. That itself was a growing experience for me.

Now I see those days as a learning curve, we, meaning each man and woman, had to go through for their personal growth. I am grateful for these lessons I could learn from, and most importantly, I am very proud of myself for having had the strength and wisdom to not succumb to all the lies that they wanted us to buy into, like the PCR and Vax being good for us. This is the main thing I take from 2020 until now.

These past years we have lived have been very intense on the personal and planetary body for each human, it has helped to raise awareness and accelerate a growth of consciousness within each man and woman worldwide. Many have awoken and opened their eyes kind of overnight by all that has happened, beginning to question life itself, going deep into research and really looking within, as all that we live externally, was created by us, we get this opportunity to dwell into our minds, beliefs, patterns to see why we have created it in first place.

Remember that everything, really, all is created by us, even the toughest experiences and lessons. When we learn to understand to see it from this perspective, life begins to flow and widens your horizon, we take accountability for ourselves and our actions, stop blaming others outside of us.

When we go back to the beginning of humanity, learn or reconnect with the law of ONE and Unity consciousness and see that there have always been wars and splits amongst races fighting for control, we get asked by our higher selves to walk and act in the opposite direction, to remain centred in our hearts and sort all we live from within, it is a lesson when we understand this. If some intend to break our Spirit by outer circumstances, we get to revert it all by using our inner resources to ascend on our inner Krystal spiral, activate all the dormant DNA strands and open our inner Spheres, which are equal to dimensions.

Each of us holds the original 12 D blueprints within, containing the codes and keys, fire letters and more to return to the Avatar self which we are organically. Once we manage that, we cannot be influenced by others wanting to control humanity, as we have then regained all our wisdom and sacredness which makes us the divine Angelic Human that we are by default, by birthright, and our light shines so bright that it overrides any false light. It activates others that surround you too, accelerating the process for all to return to their true self.

Do continue to stand strong in your pillar of light, no matter what occurs outside of you, even if the bank systems are collapsing, the food and its supplies get limited/controlled, know that all this is the last attempt of the dark Agenda to still try to control mankind? Do not consent to any digital currency, get yourself prepared in buying silver or gold so you can stand sovereign and not depend on anyone else. Unite with your tribe, your Soul family where you all will thrive in harmony, being sustained by what Mother nature provides.

I feel mankind is being led back to nature, back to organic ways of living, creating jointly wonderful places to be in peace and in pure connection with Earth again. All this technology and AI out there, has given humans too much to know and too much to think about. Life is not about knowing nor thinking, it is all about feeling and living in sacredness, in connection with the Source and in connection with Mother nature in accordance with the order of life itself.

We are the Guardians of the Earth and must learn or remember to live in order with its Spirit, treating Mother Earth well, not exploiting her and the wonderful resources she contains, they belong to her, not to us, to be used and transmuted into technology, etc. She has always provided everything we needed, but we have abused of her goods and the consequences are dangerous now as the rivers are drying, the forests are being deforested, the entire climate is changing due to it and it is affecting us, something we are seeing worldwide. It is about returning to simplicity, caring and respecting Mother Earth. Learn how to live in harmony with her again.

Did you know that the waters of Mother Earth are us, the woman? Did you know that the carbon inside the Earth is her lungs? Imagine what happens if all that is being destroyed? Do you realize that by exploiting her, we are extinguishing ourselves? We don't even need any dark Agenda in play for that, we do it to ourselves!

I wish we could all learn to be more mindful and reconnect with our own inner sacredness and Spirit, as all we need is there for us. It's about simplicity, returning to a simple life. We were thought to have a lot, to gain and accumulate material stuff we do not need, accumulate in our minds, bodies and spirit even. That all is excess baggage we carry along in our lives, pulling us down, weighing on us, making us unhappy and miserable, even creating a cycle of wanting more, being greedy and addicted to the consumer world.

This behaviour keeps us looping in repetitive circles in our lower chakras which are also the 1st, 2nd and 3rd dimensions preventing us from living from our heart (4th dimension) to climb higher in the Krystal Spiral, the organic living 12D tree of life. Many humans live and circle only in those dimensions, but we must break through it if we want mankind to thrive. Now is exactly that time, the Universe has given this chance to all men and women, since we are in the Ascension cycle. Open your eyes, your mind, your third eye, your heart, your consciousness and grow, by doing this, you already help mankind. Life itself is so very beautiful and goes by in a blink of an eye, make the most of it, laugh, be joyful, lovable, compassionate, humble, share, give and be open to receive too, love yourself and each other human and living species. They all have a soul too, feel and connect to nature.

Do the inner work, freeing yourself from pain, suffering, memories we hold from our Ancestors and other lifetimes and begin to heal within. I have done this this year 2023, every month going deep within, healing stuff which does no longer serve my highest timeline, my highest path and outcome, my highest mission and purpose, and guys, you know what - it feels so very freeing and amazing to let go of all the weight of the world we sometimes carry for lifetimes on our shoulders.

Then, you become lighter in all aspects of your life. You become happy again, vibrant and regain all the positive aspects of yourself which were buried under beliefs, patterns and programs running through you.

I live in constant awe with life and its beauty, guided by the Universe taking me to the right place where I am meant to be in each now moment. When you align heart-mind-spirit in coherence, balanced with inner peace, it happens automatically that you get to do what you have come here for, live your purpose. I feel so privileged to be an old Soul, to help raise the frequencies on the Planet and beyond, to connect with Source and be aligned with all that is, the Law of ONE.

This month I feel so fortunate getting to travel to a location, we are a group of 12 men and women, who will activate an ancient site, crystal pyramids under the sea, to bring them back to its purity and clear out all the reversals and inorganic energies running there still. This will help liberate humankind even more, all will feel it in their being, and like that, step by step, the organic is being restored in this world and beyond. Energy work is very powerful, more so when one unites with a group of individuals doing the same thing. Each hold different keys and codes, come from different race linages, carry a unique flame with its ray and frequency. This combined, has an immense power for all and when done and commanded, takes place and expands through all gridlines, all DNA, all dimensions, realities, time and space and through the zero point field. It will be perceived by many, received by all, knowingly or unknowingly.

This all happens once you reclaim your sacredness and do the inner work; you too will be guided to do what your Soul chose to come here for in this lifetime.

Other than that, I really enjoy listening to what my higher self has in store for me, communicating and listening to it is the most helpful tool we all do have. It will help you in all the above-mentioned, leading you to be where you are meant to be in each now moment, fully supported and protected. I get to travel down to south Spain soon to visit family, visiting Portugal as they live by the Portuguese Border, I travelled to Switzerland earlier this year to see my sons and most probably get to travel to Columbia soon as well, to reconnect with an ancient tribe of which I feel strongly I was part of in other lifetimes. There I will learn furthermore amazing things leading me into being even more myself in Oneness with all that is.

Do trust beloved Soul, that whatever is happening here on Planet Earth and in your experience is just right for you, don't fight it, look within as how it makes you feel, then stand strong and tall in your sovereign pillar of light and keep moving in the direction your higher self and your teams or spirit guides tell you, that will eventually bring you onto your most aligned path and give you a wonderful sense of fulfillment, macro to micro and micro to macro. Learn to be you again, to touch trees and connect with their spirit, speak with the waters and the rocks, whisper to the animal and elemental kingdoms and listen to what they have to say to you, all, and anything you receive, is an answer to your questions and a message for you. Ask your guides to lead you, help you, there is no one better than them to guide you each moment, each step, each second. Slowly you will reconnect with the simplicity of life, the most beautiful things are simple and accessible from within, it's like a subtle bridge of faith and trust. Allow the frequency of Love to be your main guide in life for each action you take, for each decision you make, give thanks to all that is and before you sleep at night and awake in the morning, give thanks for your sacred breath and heartbeat, gifting you another moment to experience in this limitless wheel of consciousness growth and expansion.

If you are in a relationship with a partner, say good night in peace, do not carry resentment or anger into the dreamworld, forgive before you close your eyes and express your truth to them from your sacred heart space. Speak from your perspective without accusing, blaming, simply express how you feel, from your truthful heart center filled with love, then there is no way they get into a defensive reaction. You have expressed your truth.

Do the same with all family members, friends, hold no secrets, express them freely, no matter how deep or painful they have been, it is liberating your clan and will not be passed onto the next generation then to be healed still, do as much inner work as possible to help free mankind. As you do this, you free and heal yourself, we are ONE, the other is only your mirror reflecting yourself back at you, everything that you are, your love, anger, etc. As you heal yourself, you heal Mother Earth and the Universe, Multiverse and Omniverse and we all unite in love, peace, purity, humbleness, compassion, truth and genuine authenticity.

When you come to the conclusion that all we believed ourselves to be, all we believed to have learned, we realize that it all needs to be unlearned and reverted because most of it was based on false structures, beliefs, concepts, values not aligned for our highest path, having installed fears in our minds which sit deep in our subconscious level and can take lifetimes to unravel; then only do you start to believe you are beautiful as a soul and being and you are worthy of infinite limitless blessings and happenings in your life, that all and anything is possible to archive and once you overcome all that you believed initially to be correct, it feels extremely rewarding and fills you with an abundance on all levels. You rest in a state of inner wellbeing, where your Central Nervous System is no longer under fight flight mode or in survival, but in an ever-flowing state of Bliss and harmony, attracting and manifesting with ease and grace anything you desire for your highest timeline.

When we allow the Ego to step aside and let consciousness run the game we call life, things fall into places you would have never imagined. Savour each experience, even if it feels hard or dense, remember it all serves a purpose and is a disguised blessing and a wonderful lesson to give thanks for, to explore what it means for you. This is what we all choose on a Soul level before we incarnate into our vehicle called body, it's the vehicle for our consciousness we need to nourish and care for, so that consciousness can continue to work through you for more experiences. Your station of identity, which is you with the name you hold in this lifetime, only wants to experience different lessons we choose before we arrive here. None is good nor bad, they simply are experiences and as your Soul evolves each lifetime and learns from them, we will choose less and less dense experiences and our Soul grows wiser, until we eventually get the chance to choose if we wish to reincarnate and help mankind ascend even more since there will always be young Souls needing guidance here wanting to experience lessons which we may have already gone through. This is how sacred life is beloved Soul!

May these words carry you into your heart and ignite a fire for life, a fire for love and a fire for inspiration to flow and be in simplicity and connected to all that you are and ever were. I greet you from my sacred heart to yours with LOVE.

## Peter English

It didn't really end, did it? I don't recall a news bulletin informing us that it's officially over, that there's no more danger and we can get on with our lives now. When exactly was the end of isolation? It just fizzled out without too much fuss or notification and the usual lack of guidance from the Government telling us it's safe to go out and mingle, party or travel.

There was nothing like the mandatory misery they imposed upon us at the beginning when lockdown started on that definitive date. Bang! Lockdown! No, just a solemn nothingness! There was a brief period of time when mask wearing was still compulsory on public transport and then that ended too. I remember that we still had to wear a mask at the doctors, in a hospital, or at the pharmacy but then we started noticing people not wearing masks even though nobody told us the pandemic was over.

If they had, we might have celebrated with national or international celebrations with fiestas and street parties. Relationships and communities are so important, after all being with others is one of the keys to happiness but more importantly, we needed to learn how to make things better again for us all.

Some good things came from lockdown. One was the amount of inspiration and innovation, people adapted very quickly and became much more resourceful. More and more people started working from home, do people really need to go to the office? Zoom flourished with the rapid increase in demand for online meetings and many restaurants offered takeaways when they hadn't previously. Apps for food deliveries were everywhere!

The planet certainly had a breather and rested, maybe it recovered momentarily, but two years in our long history is a very short time, almost negligible.

On the downside, is the continued use of QR codes in restaurants. Grrr, it annoys me. I understand their use and I get the convenience (for the restaurant) but it seems some eateries are reluctant to give them up now lockdown is over. Personally, I like a menu in my hands. The same applies to fiddly little packets of salt, pepper, butter packs, sugar, vinegar and olive oil. "Seriously, hey guys, don't you know it's over!" Give me a salt and pepper grinder, a bowl of sugar and bottles with oil and vinegar any time and a menu I can hold in my hands.

I had to laugh, I was on a flight recently and queuing at the gate where you scan your boarding pass – there are no operatives anymore – was a sign illustrating keeping your distance, one and a half metres from anybody else. Yes, OK, we can comply there, where there's plenty of space, but in the airport lounge, people are hustled and bustled together. Then there's the plane itself, the queue to board with people pressing up behind you, in front of you, to the side of you. Those with backpacks are the worst (that includes me by the way!) and then you sit in rows stuffed in like tinned sardines. What a joke!

In the second book of this trilogy, I referred to the sensational news about coronavirus and the fear it created, the daily death toll, the warnings about masks, gloves and sanitisers. Avoid shaking hands, just do the clenched fists thing, certainly no kissing, caressing or cuddling. Social distancing – who on earth coined that phrase! Looking back, I think how dare they, or more to the point, how could they enforce these mandatory lockdown rules, which created so  much misery, destroyed people's lives and ruined the economy? Well, this goes to prove they can, they did and most probably, will do again. We are still hearing of new variants with yet other weird names. So what next? Is jabbing us up to the eyeballs the answer? Is complying with these rules the answer?

Since the last book, I've met so many people who refused the vaccination, more and more of them.

I'm honestly surprised at the number of people who kept quiet about it, probably for good reason, after all, the unvaccinated were blamed for spreading the virus and making everybody else sick! I know lots of people who, when they get ill, are sicker now than they used to be before Covid and when they get ill, they appear to have Covid type symptoms – bronchial coughing, severe aching, lack of energy, loss of taste and smell, but worse is pulmonary issues, thrombosis and breathing difficulties. These are usually people who tested positive and had the virus irrespective of being vaccinated. This indicates to me that once having had the virus, the person is more vulnerable as it seems to leave a weakness that a later infection latches on to. I have no scientific proof of this, it's just my observation. I also question whether vaccinated people are more susceptible to the above symptoms than the unvaccinated.

Lockdown didn't affect me too much personally, life goes on here in Spain as it does everywhere, there are chores to do in the villa, we are travelling quite a bit and last June 2022, we got involved in a plan to sail a yacht from Denia in Spain to Levkas, Greece. We knew two of the other couples who were interested in participating and as a result, we took it in turns sailing from here to the Balearic islands, Sardinia, Corsica, Elba, down the coast of Italy to Rome and then the Amalfi coast, down to the Aeolian Island just north of Sicily.

It has been the most wonderful sailing experience ever, we saw places we never knew existed, such as the Maddalena Islands between Sardinia and Corsica. What a gem of a beautiful and peaceful setting, I would go back in a heartbeat. We ended up in a tranquil bay nestled between three islands but unbeknownst to us, mooring overnight was prohibited, we were not supposed to be there so we had the whole place to ourselves! The water was crystal clear and a morning swim to a tiny beach was enjoyed by all.

We would not have been able to attempt such a trip during lockdown and it's amazing what the possibilities are now since that time.

Putting it into context, we wouldn't have been able to travel with all the restrictions, so imagine all the boats and yachts that were not chartered at that time, the loss of business is just incredible - and that's just one tiny type of holiday business.

People think living in Spain, that we go to the beach everyday, sit in the sun and sip piña coladas. In fact we never go to the beach, only when family or friends come. I've retired four times – and I'm still working! We're involved in holiday rentals, Tanya is pretty good on the online letting platforms and little by little, we built up a good reputation, not only with British clients but Spanish, Dutch, French – you name it. While she deals with the admin, I'm Mr Fix It. I mend toilets, hinges, door handles, locks, I'm a pool cleaner, a gardener, a plasterer and painter/decorator but my favourite task (not!) is replacing gas bottles. It's very common here in Spain, every property uses butane for either the domestic cooker or the gas barbecues. They always need changing and it's a proverbial pain in the backside. Then furniture gets damaged or broken, light bulbs need replacing – the list is endless but hey ho!

We are the more fortunate ones, we have a house and an income. We're not rich but all in all, we enjoy a reasonably comfortable lifestyle - but what about those who were deeply affected by the lockdown, families in crisis, those with dependents, with special needs, those with increased financial constraints if they couldn't work or weren't allowed to go to work unless they were vaccinated? The lockdown caused terrible rifts between family members creating arguments and disagreements. What about the elderly, the sick and the lonely who couldn't even have visitors? People couldn't visit their loved ones or worse still, attend funerals. Can you imagine going to a Zoom wedding or funeral?

Then there are issues with mental health. Not everyone is strong, some are anxious, some have debilitating health anxiety. People can survive a certain amount of turmoil and instability in a crisis when it happens and a few days or a week later it's over, but when the unknown drags on and on for months and even years, these traumatic events can and probably did cause clinical levels of PTSD (Post Traumatic Stress Disorder) and apparently although the psychological challenges of Covid are huge, these issues aren't being addressed at all. It's the same old story, investment in mental health is extremely poor.

At the beginning of this year 2023, we lost a cat, poor Lola. She adopted us four years ago at Christmas when she arrived on our driveway with Ximo. We named them, you could tell Ximo had once been someone's pet but Lola was half feral although everywhere Ximo went, Lola went too. She would never come in the house, in fact neither of them are what I call 'good value' cats, they don't like to be touched, you can't pick them up, they certainly won't sit on your lap.

Lola started to get very thin, she just wouldn't eat, this went on for weeks, she was so emaciated poor thing and eventually, when she was weak enough that I could catch her by scooping her up in an old towel, I took her to the vets. They put her on a drip overnight, rehydrated her and said they couldn't find anything wrong with her.

She'd been anaesthetised and as she came round, I opened the door of the cat box and she bolted out across the garden, wobbling on her way and we never saw her again. She completely disappeared. I fear she went off to die somewhere; it was so sad.

I wondered if animals catch our viruses but then some years ago, I'd been to a talk about health vs disease (dis-ease) and the doctor giving the talk focused on viruses. One thing stuck in my mind and I remember he explained that viruses do not pass from one species to another, he said not only are viruses 'animal specific' but they are 'organ specific' too. If this is the case humans cannot 'catch' a virus from bats, or pigs - remember swine flu? So what is this nonsense they feed us?

So no, poor Lola did not die of Covid, probably some feline illness, but sadly she is no longer with us. Did your pet - your dog, cat, horse or stick-insect get sick and die of Covid? No, of course not, it's never going to happen! Bats in Wuhan, honestly!

Life goes on, I do fear for the near future, the next pandemic, I'm convinced there will be one and probably quite soon. There are so many discussions about where coronavirus came from and why. We'll never know the answers because of corruption and hush-ups, the truth is out there but there are no admissions or apologies. We know flu-type viruses mutate, but come on, not this much in such a short space of time, causing such debilitating illness and death?

We have learned that scientists have now proven that the mRNA jabs were not proper vaccinations and didn't work.

We also know that all sorts of information – even the vaccine's inventor's name - has been erased from history books and that patents were taken out for coronavirus vaccines some nine or ten years before the pandemic. There is factual evidence of this, so the question is why?

Did they know it was coming and better still, was it done deliberately?

You have to do your own research and draw your own conclusions.

It's all out there if you are sufficiently interested. It's your health and your life so you should be. Do your research, look stuff up, investigate people – doctors, scientists, journalists, pharmaceutical companies, financial companies, company bosses and owners, the big worldwide players, even MPs and governments.

Dig deep. Join groups both online and physically!

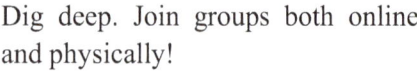

# Julia Evans

We cannot change the past or predict the future; all we have ownership of is the present moment.

I struggled to write these words, thinking back to lockdown, trying to sum it up. How it affected others, how it affected me, what I learned, what we all learned. I have no answers, only questions...

It is too easy to let our past experiences affect how we view the future. The coronavirus changed the world, it changed us as individuals... or did it? Perhaps it just showed us who we really are...

So many layers, such a complex subject. So much confusion. How much of the truth will we ever know, and what is the truth? Is there only one truth, or are we just living through a kaleidoscope of different beliefs, different perspectives?

Who can we trust?

Listening to the experts - their perspectives hold more weight - but what happens when the experts have vastly different opinions? Do our own perspectives, our own past experiences influence who we listen to?

Some experts hold more power than others, more power to control and change the lives of many - but does that mean that their truth, their opinion is correct?

If I had to sum up the entire experience, it would be that we are searching for the truth. This is my truth, what I saw and felt, and maybe you, the reader, can relate to some of this. I will attempt to unpack the complex layers and emotions of what lockdown and Covid meant to me. Some are conflicting, but in each moment, they were my truth. Looking at these concepts, I hope that wherever you stood, whatever your opinion/truth/perspectives were, there is some common ground. Core values that ran through our experience as a collective. Inviting you to the concept that we are all one. That on some level, we all experienced the same...

**Freedom -**
We all felt as though we lost a level of freedom. Did this show us how important freedom is? We were unable to leave our house as and when we wanted, unable to decide whether to wear a mask or not, unable to work freely. Some felt they lost their freedom because the choice of what they inject into their body was taken away, while others were filled with fear that they would get sick if they left the house.

Some felt our freedom was taken in the sense that we were not allowed to trust ourselves, our own instincts, trust our bodies. Some felt their freedom was taken because others were not abiding by the rules - risking their health. Either way, we were forced to place our autonomy in the hands of others. Either way we all felt a lack of freedom - a fundamental human right. This led to anger...

**Anger and Conflict -**
Anger that we had lost control, anger that others' actions (those in power that held the keys to a locked door, or the person at the bus stop refusing to wear a mask) were constraining who we wanted to be. I believe that anger is a cover emotion for fear...

**Fear -**
So much fear. Fear of a virus, fear of a vaccine, fear of losing an income, fear of loneliness, fear of not seeing loved ones, fear that our child would be forced to wear a mask, fear of our Grandma's vulnerability, fear of the power held by pharmaceutical companies, fear of our own mortality, FEAR OF WHAT THE FUTURE WILL BRING:

We were all scared of different things, but we were all scared. None of this was our fault; we were the victims...

**Victim Consciousness -**
We can never control the actions of others; we can only control how we react to them. All that I know who work in the spiritual and personal development world have an understanding of Victim consciousness - taking radical responsibility for our actions/ thoughts and feelings - understanding that we have the power to create our lives, that all that happens around us is a reflection of what is inside of us. As far as I could see it, the whole experience was the biggest test for us - can we step forward with love and kindness, the deep knowing that we are all one? With so much fear, it was not easy work... Can we truly integrate our spiritual

practices in such difficult times... and where do you even begin? For me, the answer is, if in doubt, always start with Gratitude...

**Gratitude -**
Stop and take a moment to smell the roses.
Gratitude was a huge part of the whole experience of lockdown and coming out, and it led me to appreciate so many small things that I took for granted. My main one was spending time with my children, but I was also deeply grateful for my body, my health, my house. I hold a lot of gratitude for the whole experience, and if we really take the time to pause and look, there is always something to be grateful for.

I remember the first day the children were allowed out to play - the simple act of going to the end of the road with my young son on his tricycle - I saw a profound beauty in this simple act, so much so that it reduced me to tears. How often had I sat in parks with my sons, longing for the playtime to end, distracted by what I had to do at home. I had lost the potent magic of simply watching a child play outside. There is so much magic around us that we are desensitised to. But during Covid, I felt an underlying ripple of gratitude and appreciation for the small things. The big question is, have we remembered this?

**Peace -**
I cannot deny that, along with feeling fear and anger, frustration and confusion, I also felt a sense of peace - especially in lockdown. For the first time in so many years, I had the opportunity to STOP, to step off the hamster wheel that is so many of our lives. How often do we say yes to things that we do not really want to do? Covid had, in all respects, given us a giant excuse to say NO... and whether it was an excuse that was forced upon us, or later on a choice, it was accepted. I think many of us felt the opportunity to

pause and take a breath and the realisation that it had been a long time since we were able to do that...

**LOVE -**
In amongst the chaos, the conflict, I saw so much LOVE and kindness. I saw the love between family members on Zoom calls, I saw the kindness in the person who takes a bag of shopping and leaves it at the door for the person too scared to leave the house. I saw the tenderness of a first embrace as loved ones were reunited. To quote a rather cliché yet beloved Christmas film (forgive me), LOVE ACTUALLY IS EVERYWHERE...

I invite you to think again of truth, our search for truth, and I ask you kindly to contemplate the following statement: Perhaps there is only one truth... and that is LOVE.

Nobody knows what the future holds; we have no control over what it will bring. The sole aspect we can influence is how we respond to each moment that unfolds before us. At our core, who do we aspire to be? Can we step forward with love, gratitude, and compassion? Can we embrace the understanding that perhaps there is no single 'right' way, only diverse viewpoints? Recognising that, at our very core as humans, we all share the same journey, the same emotions, and that our opinions and perspectives are nothing but minor details.

Trust - we have to trust - and not necessarily in the opinions of others, expert or not...

All we can do is learn to trust ourselves.

# Hayley

Over the autumn and winter of 2022/2023, since writing my last story, life seemed to go on in much the same way. Luckily restrictions and masks didn't come back. Things didn't seem too bad for everyone, though I think more people seemed to be getting health issues which we wonder if linked to the jabs.

Jabbing older and vulnerable people continued and I'd hear people saying they'd been for their 5th and 6th boosters which just seems crazy to me; to keep getting a jab for something that doesn't stop you catching it or passing it on was its purpose. Some people seem to be catching Covid as many times as the number of jabs they've had. I still don't think I've had it.

As I write we are starting to hear about Covid cases rising again - in August in the middle of summer! I only know of people who've had the jab catching it again. We also hear that all school aged children will have the flu jab this year whereas normally its only very young children, the elderly and the vulnerable; it does seem ridiculous and people in the 'truth movement' think that this will cause a spike in illness and maybe deaths in children creating panic that there is a new virus. Indeed, as expected, there are reports about another new strain, more fear, more propaganda.

Apparently, some movie sets are already enforcing mask wearing again.

'ULEZ' - Ultra Low Emission Zone, restricting people driving into city centres, and '15 minute cities' - making sure all necessary amenities are within a 15 minute walk, have already been introduced in some areas. Some people are unaware of them and the way they are presented to us sounds lovely but the reality of living with these restrictions will be shocking.

Next it could be using pollution and climate change measures as another excuse and reason to put restrictions on us. I don't believe we are going through a climate change and there are hundreds of scientists who have spoken out against climate change and explained that the earth goes through cycles where it heats up and cools down over thousands of years or more, and that actually we are in a cold period right now. Just look at the UK weather, it's been very unsettled with no extremes of heat in summer or cold in winter. I think the climate crisis is just another way for us to be controlled and isn't about saving the planet at all. As usual those creating the rules and talking about climate change travel around by private jet and fuel-guzzling cars, whilst telling us to go electric or cut our emissions.

People living in Hawaii, where they recently had the catastrophic fires, were sharing stories and footage saying that trees hadn't burnt, but cars and houses destroyed. Footage shows Directed Energy Weapons could have been the cause and I've seen numerous videos from a few years back showing information where there was talk about needing the land in Maui and how to get it from official sources, so it really makes you wonder if it was deliberate and a land grab.

The strain on the economy from the lockdowns and furloughs is another worry. We see people unable to get appointments to see or register with doctors or dentists; huge waiting lists. Mortgage rates are much higher making it harder for people to get on the property ladder or afford their repayments.

In my opinion we are being pushed to give more personal information online in everything we do under the guise of keeping us safe. Another fear tactic. The way the media and TV shows portray the new restrictions makes many believe that these things are good when in reality we will be monitored and prevented from doing certain things if we don't comply, much like an episode of Black Mirror or the Dystopian 1984 book.

People use 'chip & pin' or 'tap & pay' on their cards or phones as it seems convenient rather than needing to draw out cash each time they want to buy something, but the more we use these methods and not cash the more companies will stop letting us pay by cash. It's already happening.

We need to keep using cash and encourage others to do so too. In Canada last year when truckers were protesting people sent them money through a website, GoFundMe or similar; the website stopped the money from getting to the truckers because the government disagreed with what they were doing. Our every move can be controlled when everything is digital. We can be stopped from spending money as and when and how we want to and withdrawing our money from our bank account can be restricted. It's already happening.

We need to keep using cash and encourage others to do so too.

The last 6 months have brought a lot of change into my life. Finding love is hard enough in this modern world where people are using dating apps and everything seems superficial and short term, with swipe right and then ghosting, fickle people, busy people, distance and much more. And then to want to find someone who is on the same page as you regarding the pandemic, Covid jabs and not trusting the media and governments! You also want to make sure that you have the same values and beliefs and fundamental wishes - do they want children and marriage?

It would seem impossible but I did it! I found Love!

Despite there being a dating app and a couple of websites dedicated to meeting unjabbed people, it still felt like it might not be an easy task, and I can be a bit fussy at the best of times! On top of all the ticks needed in boxes, when someone did tick them all... would that person live anywhere nearby?

I tried to have some hope and belief that I would meet my match and that maybe thinking of it differently and in a more positive light would narrow my search down for me to make it easier rather than harder.

Much like when you filter your options on a website when looking for something to buy, narrowing your search down to the colour, size, style, price of an item - it helps you find what you are looking for more quickly. That was my mindset.

Even though I had not been a fan of dating apps a friend suggested to me that we both sign up at the same time in January 2023. It would be fun!

I reluctantly decided to give it another go; we would help each other out with our profiles and finding someone. I created my profile and mentioned that I was into holistic health, that I believe in body autonomy and that was about it as far as expressing my views to see if anyone picked up on it. A number of guys didn't understand so I knew they were not on my wavelength and a few did but weren't my type.

I did get chatting to one guy after a couple months of being on POF (Plenty Of Fish dating website) but he kept wasting my time, seemed too busy to organise a date and told me to keep my options open. I then decided to revamp my profile and uploaded a photo of me in my 'Resist, Defy, Do Not Comply' t-shirt.

I added a few more things to my profile to make my stance on things clear and the next day I had a message from a new guy called Armand. He sent me a longish message saying how wide awake he was, and he could tell I was too.

He sounded nice and he was definitely attractive, he didn't live too far away which was a bonus. On the second day of messaging me Armand asked me if I wanted to go for a date. I agreed as this other guy had been annoying me and Armand was making a real effort with me. He messaged me consistently, chose and booked a great restaurant in my area, not making me meet halfway between where we live. He was forthright and assertive which I found very attractive; a man taking the lead, being in his masculine and doing the planning and organising, so I knew I had to meet him to give him a chance.

A few days later, on March 17th St. Patricks Day, after finishing work I was getting ready to meet Armand and feeling a bit nervous, but telling myself that even if I don't feel a spark that at least we have our views on the last 3 years to discuss, so all would be OK.

I headed to the restaurant to meet Armand and as soon as I saw him, I felt relieved and pleased as I thought he was better looking than his photos, tall, slim, and handsome. Armand stood up to greet me and gave me a respectful peck on the cheek. We sat down and started talking effortlessly and nonstop - the waitress came over 3 times to try to take our order, yet we hadn't even looked at the menu, we were too engrossed talking. I knew that night that we were going to date. I could tell Armand was attracted to me by the way he listened intently, leaned across the table giving me his full attention and had amazing eye contact. I felt pretty excited and smitten afterwards with how well we got on instantly, The nonstop talking, and finding out about each other, and all I found out about him was just what I was looking for. I was very attracted to him and his energy and was sure I would see him again. The next day he messaged me to say he'd love to see me again and sent me his number - we arranged to meet the following weekend and started to message daily.

Within a few dates I knew I wanted him to be my life partner and felt that he wanted the same. The last 6 months have been amazing, the more I get to know Armand, the time we spend together and the plans we make for the future make me love him more and know I've met the right guy. We knew early on that we had the same views and values on many things, and we discussed important topics like the way we want to bring up children; this made me feel we have a strong foundation for a lasting relationship which I am excited to be in.

Meeting Armand has changed my life!

I never thought I would meet someone so well suited to me, but as many of my friends and family have said, he's my perfect match, and definitely a great apocalypse partner. Meeting Armand has exceeded my expectations of meeting someone online who is so right for you.

Since meeting we have done so much... met each other's friends, enjoyed a 9-day road trip around France, been to a Vegan festival, 3 weddings and he's met most of my family. Next, we are off to Latvia to meet his family.

I am excited for our future and how it's developing - we hope to move in together within a year and at some point, have children too. Knowing I have Armand I feel less worried about the future, because I know it's something we will figure out together - as long as we have each other life will be happier, and easier to navigate - we can face whatever the future brings - TOGETHER!

## Jacob RA Dodds

New Earth starts with each One of us.

Through the mist of the awakening shadows, there is a light. A light of the collective who are awakening to all that they are.

Knowing, for one to walk in light, one must journey through their shadows. A journey that is so rewarding and joyous, one wouldn't want to miss.

This journey is said to be one of the longest, although it is of a short distance. This journey is from the egoic mind to the bountiful loving heart.

It is of great wonder and awe, to be living from the bountiful loving heart. From the heart, we see life through the eyes of the soul and feel the rhythms of our innate nature. The nature of being human, the nature of our dear Mother Earth, the nature of light and shadow, the nature of our presence with all that is.

Here, we begin to relate to life with an innerstanding of a creative force beyond all of what is happening around us. We see more clearly and choose where to engage and where to take a breath, and walk away.

There is much that can be said about what is happening on Earth, to the planet itself, within our communities and for ourselves. By walking away, it's not about being ignorant or ignoring things, nor is it about condoning other people's actions and ways of being. It is about keeping it simple. Simple being, me taking full responsibility for what and where I am putting my energy. From which place am I adding to the collective field of existence - the egoic mind or the bountiful loving heart?

We are creators, and we are being asked to create the world we wish to see as though it is here now. To do this, we have to know who we truly are, and to know who we truly are, is Sovereignty.

Sovereignty is a beautiful gift, we are all worthy of. We experience this through getting in touch with ourselves in a deep intimate way.

Through this love of ourselves, we create such profound experiences and relationships with each other. We get to co-create on a purposeful level and assist Mother Earth and each other in ways beyond comprehension. To know ourselves in such an intimate way, we need to feel. Feel what the body is communicating with us. To learn through feeling the body, not from the mind.

To sit and listen. To let go of what no longer serves us and have a death of the old self, to create space for the higher frequencies of our being to come into the body.

This is the ascension process, because ascension happens through our body and the body of Mother Earth. As we ascend, we get to know ourselves as the amazing multi-dimensional beings we are. By staying grounding and present, we anchor in, what is here for the highest good of All.

So as we heal our waters, we heal Mother Earth's waters, such is the deep connection we have. It's like this, because we birthed this life through her. There is no separation.
We are One.

As we rise, so does she, and vice versa.

The more we rise individually and as a collective, the more love and beauty we will see. The more light will be felt and nothing outside of us can touch us anymore.

We go through a purifying experience and this can bring things to the surface to be looked at, felt, loved and released, along with our true codex and original angelic human blueprint coming into being.

With this embodiment of purification we all become crystalline. No shadows, just pure light and love. Crystallized.

Are you ready to be Crystal-real-lized?

Come, hold my hand and we will walk together.

# Joe

*written many years ago but has relevance to today

## Silence

Hold your silence for another day,
There's gotta be another way to go
Look outside it's another day,
They've come to steal your life away,
Your life away... then your soul goes with it
This is what we say is - 'We don't need your antidote -
we don't need your pain.'

*Joe*

Look outside it's another day,
With everybody screaming out loud,
It's another day, it's another day.
It's a day to make a stand,
It's a day to make demands,
to make them listen to us.
This is what we say is - 'We don't need your antidote -
we don't need your pain.'

How did we get here,
well we'd come so far
then the darkness came
were we the ones to blame
going back in time we ignore the signs
all of the freedom we shamefully wasted.

Tell me changes that you have made,
make me believe we're saved,
and freedom's all your asking
Look around this brand new day,
have all the bad things gone away,
have they gone away
you bet your life they haven't.

# Conclusion

Looking back over the past three years I see what a roller coaster we have been on and as we head towards the end of 2023 we have started to see very different energies throughout the world. There is the ongoing energy of Destruction and Division and we pray daily for those caught up unwillingly within this - but - we are also seeing Unity and Unlimited Creativity among many people. The initiatives are fantastic in local communities across the world; people coming together to talk about creating new opportunities, doing things differently, new projects, forming different systems  including health, farming and education, and saying 'no' to things they consider to be unreasonable or just plain wrong.

Although we are connected across the world as never before via the internet and social media, in many ways we've never been so disconnected. It's a time for reflection, how we make things right remembering that collectively we are strong. More money in the world and less happiness - trillions made by the few from wars and indeed the recent lockdowns. An abundance of pharmaceutical drugs and many more sick people. Pharmaceutical companies making trillions on the drugs and their side effects that many die from, including the vaccine market.

In my World, my Vision, the World I want for my children and grandchildren, for your children and grandchildren, for our future generations... there will be - LOVE - Truth - Justice - Freedom - Trust - Peace - Harmony - Forgiveness - Equality - Acceptance - Community - Fairness - everyone will be heard. A world where we value the children of the world and respect our elders for the wisdom they hold. It's not hard, it's actually really simple if we all follow basic rules and put an end to the hamster wheel we're on with wars, and consistently being encouraged to hate on anyone who is a different colour or has a different culture, opinion etc... I know I'm not alone and we are heading in the right direction.

My filter system is much more advanced than when we started off in 2020. By that I mean, having started questioning what was going on back in 2020, I now question everything. I can more easily spot a lie or propaganda at a distance! My BS filter. I'm not always right but I'm getting pretty good!

I choose to live with unlimited dreams for our future. I think these severe times are here to encourage us to dig deeper and realise that things weren't as we wanted them and we now have an opportunity to make changes, to thrive, not just survive.

Since doing an interview with the wonderful Richard Vobes back in July, I have received correspondence from people across the world thanking me for recording the individual and unique memories of ordinary people living through these times and encouraging me to continue recording the written word so that it can never be forgotten. So I will continue.

Thank you to my old and new friends for joining me in Book 3 and, as always, I'm sorry I didn't have room for all the stories that have been sent to me. I will continue writing and logging and I will start featuring stories on my website as more and more people share their experiences.
*If you would like to share your memories of the lockdown years please contact me via my website www.memoriesoflockdown.com

And so, for another year, I leave you with my prayers and positive thoughts and with my optimism, encouragement and heartfelt thanks for those of you committed to making our world a better place.

See you next year!

'The best way to predict the future is to create it'

'WE are the change'

## *Topics being discussed as we go to print at the end of October 2023:*

War Israel/Hamas - UK PM Rishi Sunak tells Israel 'we want you to win' - Jewish protestors in D.C. demand Israel-Gaza ceasefire - Huge protests across Europe for ceasefire, negotiations & peace - people in power trading Defense stocks while shaping military policy.

Councils in the UK facing bankruptcy - mis-management of funds including bad failed investments in solar farms? What will they blame it on? Do your own research.
Whatever the reason - who will pick up the bill?

20% of people/families in the UK using food banks.

Vaccines - still being promoted in the UK - some are having them and others are choosing not to. Some regret having them and are finding protocols to rid the body of them. Some are damaged as a result of having them and seeking compensation.
Excess deaths after the rollout of COVID-19 vaccinations, nationally and internationally are not being investigated.

Andrew Bridgen pleads for an independent investigation into excess deaths - spoke to an empty chamber December 2022 and nearly a year on in October 2023. Democracy?
The question is being asked: - 'safe and effective - what does this actually mean?'

IHR - International Health Regulations - an instrument of international law, providing an overarching legal framework that defines countries' rights and obligations in handling public health events and emergencies.
Is this what we want?

Farming - on the one hand new ways of revolutionising how we produce food and supporting communities to buy direct from producers. - On the other hand currently farmland being given over to renewable energy leading to no room for crops, dairy, meat production and farmers under threat of losing funds if they don't comply - future plan to ration dairy & meat.
Perhaps that leads on to this...
Insect Farming - Headline ' By 2030 INSECTS could be one of our main sources of LEGAL protein' - Advertising: bugs & lab- grown meat - cricket-topped hummus - bug-based restaurants - salted ants - ground crickets - edible insects - insect farming - mealworm burgers - to save the planet the future of food is insects - insect farming industry set to be worth $8 Billion dollars by 2030 - grants being taken away from our crop and dairy farmers and given for insect farms.
Do your research - all about money and will likely be blamed on climate change - 'eat insects and save the planet.'

Intelligent Cities - smart tech to be trialled in towns and cities - cameras everywhere 'to keep you safe' - or - to track your every move.

Education - innovative and exciting new ways of educating our children, introducing useful life-skills, common sense and moral standards to return. Another vast subject - a book in itself! Suffice to say there are many creative people around the world finding and starting to implement a different way - parents voices being heard.

Health - many initiatives growing to offer a more holistic approach to healthcare, shifting the paradigm from treating disease, to creating health.

5G Towers going up - coming down/being disabled.

Eco Villages & Communities with Well-Being Centres.

Surveillance cameras everywhere - going up & coming down.

ULEZ - Ultra Low Emission Zone is an area in London, England, where an emissions standard based charge is applied to non-compliant road vehicles.

Blade Runners taking independent action against ULEZ expansion in London.

Child & Human Trafficking - doesn't make the headlines but is reported as the 2nd biggest industry after drugs, slavery is not a thing of the past – it has never been more prolific - people working relentlessly to save the children. Film 'Sound Of Freedom'.

Bankers Pushing Ahead For Digital Money.

Censorship - Freedom of Speech.

Leaders of governments across the world changing.

People's Jury.

15 Minute Cities - an urban planning concept in which most daily necessities and services, such as work, shopping, education, healthcare, and leisure can be easily reached by a 15-minute walk, bike ride, or public transit ride from any point in the city.

*Topics being discussed*

Many people now respectfully challenging their household bills. Where does the electricity and gas actually come from/who supplies it? How clean is the water? Where exactly does our council tax money go?

Another Variant / Another Lockdown.

War Ukraine / Russia.

Inflation / Interest Rates.

Vehicles - electric being promoted.

Net Zero - Climate Change - weather manipulation - crisis or natural evolution.

UK Election - who is fit to serve and represent the people?

US Election.

Open Debates & investigations - still waiting - nothing much to be heard or seen in mainstream media so for those curious to hear all sides of the story they search alternative media outlets. Thousands of doctors, virologists, experts across the world with opinions that do not coincide with government still silenced, censored.

Just announced ....Electronic Identification for every EU citizen. Face, Fingerprint & Eye scan. Will the UK follow?
Do we want this? Did we vote for this?
'They' say: The wallet has the highest level of both security and privacy. Over 500 experts in Cyber Security say it's going to make things less secure.
Mandatory for so-called Very Large Online Platforms (Facebook, Google, et al) to accept the EU digital wallet for login.

Pam Gregory - People's Health Alliance - Dr Reiner Fuellmich - Richard Vobes - Sandi Adams - Dr Sam White - People's Farming Alliance - Dolores Cahill - Andrew Bridgen - Donna Maxine White - Tarot by Janine - Tim Whild - Christiane Northrup - Neil McCoy-Ward - Jonathan Otto - Blossom Goodchild - World Council For Health - UK Column News.

Canada - a euthanasia group - MAIDHouse (Medical Assistance in Dying House) - which set up Canada's first "euthanasia house" is aiming to open similar "houses" where people can go to end their life through euthanasia throughout Canada.
The Isle of Man is set to become the first part of the British Isles to legalise assisted dying.
One in five cite loneliness as a reason to want to die.

Sexualisation of children - Sex Sweets marketed for children found to be available in supermarkets in the children's sweet section.
"Sex & Sweets go hand in hand, obviously. Both aim to make you feel good."
Does anyone think this is normal? OK? Acceptable?

There is so much more that could be added to this section of the book but how about this as a rather extraordinary, ridiculous, fantastic, exciting ... piece of 'Breaking News"...
*feel free to choose your adjective remembering 'We don't all see things the same way".
A 'Minister for Common Sense' has just been apppointed in the UK !!

www.ingramcontent.com/pod-product-compliance
Lightning Source LLC
Chambersburg PA
CBHW042132160426
43199CB00021B/2883